FINDING
Valentino

FINDING
Valentino

Four seasons in
my father's Italy

Angela Di Sciascio

VICTORY
BOOKS

VICTORY BOOKS
An imprint of Melbourne University Publishing Limited
187 Grattan Street, Carlton, Victoria 3053, Australia
mup-info@unimelb.edu.au
www.mup.com.au

First published 2011

Text design by Patrick Cannon
Typeset by Cannon Typesetting
Printed by Griffin Press, South Australia

National Library of Australia Cataloguing-in-Publication entry

Di Sciascio, Angela.

Finding Valentino: four seasons in my father's Italy/Angela Di Sciascio.

    9780522858419 (pbk.)

    9780522860269 (eBook)

    Di Sciascio, Valentino. Di Sciascio, Angela—Travel—Italy.

    Italians—Australia—Biography. Italians—Ethnic identity.
    Cooking, Italian. Italy—Social life and customs.

305.851094

For my nieces—be proud of your roots; enjoy my experiences, learn from the tales I tell and the recipes I share. I hope that through my stories you too will discover more about your grandpa, and that you will always remember him.

Mum and Dad, you are my inspiration.

Per la mia famiglia in Italia: grazie.

Contents

Acknowledgements

T HIS BOOK WOULD not have come about without the hospitality and generosity of my friends and relatives in Italy. They opened their homes, their hearts and their kitchens to me, and I will be forever grateful. Thanks go to the following and their families: Zio Alberto, Zia Rosaria, Maria Chiara, Mattia and Silvana, Domenichella, Giacinto and Madalena, Dora, Antonio and Rosalba, Nicola and Nicoletta, Antonietta and Gino, Biasetto and Giuseppina, Tiziana and Alberto, and last but not least, Enza.

It was a big move to leave the comfort of my home and the income of my work to run away to Italy for a year. Thank you to my brothers, who had to hold the fort and fill the gap that an only daughter leaves. My family has been a constant source of encouragement and support through this whole process. Thanks to my mother Joan Di Sciascio for proofing every version of the manuscript, overseeing and approving the content on behalf of my father, and giving me confidence to write. Thank you to Peter Di Sciascio, who has been a most eager fellow traveller on my journey to becoming an author.

Thank you also to the many people who have helped in the publishing of this book. Janet Jenkin was the first person to read and provide initial edits on my earliest draft. Janet was a keen test cook, along with a host of friends who provided invaluable feedback on the recipes. I must also thank Silvino Di Biase for providing detailed descriptions of his youth with my father and their migration journey, and Maria Chiara Di Sciascio for being my long-distance fact and dialect checker. Thanks must also go to Jacqui Gray, who championed my manuscript, Foong Ling Kong for enticing me with her enthusiasm and the team at MUP who helped make my words shine.

But most importantly, I must thank my father Valentino Di Sciascio. His story, his life and his character have driven this book. His disease has rendered him unable even to comprehend that this book exists, and I have been forever conscious of the responsibility I hold in publishing this book: to respect his ethnicity, his siblings, his village, his privacy and his memories. I hope I have done justice to him and his story.

A note on the recipes

THE RECIPES REPRODUCED here have come from watching my relatives and friends cook them, have been recommended to me by members of my family, or are dishes I have tasted on my travels. Most don't include precise quantities or even instructions. Often when I asked questions like, 'How much flour?' they would reply, 'Enough for the eggs.' When I asked, 'How many eggs?' they would tell me, 'Enough for the flour.' I have tried to estimate the correct portions, but where this has not been possible, dear reader, you, like me, may simply have to wing it.

Prologue

'I NEVER WANTED to be called Wally. I like Tino.'
Valentino (Wally) Di Sciascio, my father, looks
into my eyes. His are the piercing blue of the Abruzzese
and speak louder than his words. He looks vulnerable,
utterly honest. He is revealing something from deep
within and the sheer relief is apparent. I in turn feel
as if the whole identity of my father, Wally, Wal, is
crumbling in front of me. I don't know how to respond.
Part of me is so deeply sad for this proud man who
has carried a name he doesn't like for over fifty-five
years. Part of me feels as if my image of my father is
collapsing like a house of cards under the weight of
his sorrow.

It's difficult to explain what the name Wally means
to my family, our friends and relatives. We have never
called our father 'Dad'; he has always been Wal. All

1

our friends refer to my father as Wal. He spent many years building a family business through the toil of his labour and the honesty of his heart. He was a respected tradesman and all who dealt with him knew him as Wal. My brothers' friends would call Wal for help in the middle of the night instead of their own dads. Wal would be called on to help settle disputes with his reason and his calm nature. Wal would rise before dawn and drive the boys of the neighbourhood in his ute (piled high with surfboards, wetsuits and eager teenagers) to their favourite surf spots down the Great Ocean Road. Wal the peacemaker. Wal the loyal servant. Wal the pacifist. Wal the inventor. Wal the engineer. Wal the decent. Wal the battler. Wal, my father.

What does it mean to live with a name you don't like? Confusion weighs down on my shoulders and my heart aches. Wal the strong, loyal, tolerant, proud and good man is only part of the man before me. There is another looking at me through those eyes—Valentino. Valentino, my father.

My father's revelation is tough on our family. Moments like these are increasing. My father's Alzheimer's has released a deep-seated honesty and truth-telling in him that at times shocks, hurts, confuses and saddens us. The disease has opened a door through which he can let out all the actions and deeds of the past that have hurt him, like freeing birds from a cage. Sometimes the stories come out in waves, with emotion, tears and anger.

For those who have to listen it is heartbreaking to hear and it is hardest of all for my mother. Alzheimer's has freed him of the burden of holding in these memories any more. It has relieved him of the stiff upper lip required by our society. We all carry memories of hurt and betrayal deep inside us. For some these life lessons make them stronger. For others they become the building blocks of insecurities and weaknesses. My father had locked his away, thinking they would never be spoken of. But now he can't help it. His disease speaks for him.

I am losing my father. The man who never got angry gets angry. The man who never showed any stubbornness has become stubborn, at times like a child. The man who always told long-winded stories, always with a wise moral, now tells none. The man who never demanded now demands. The man who had to spit on his dry, cracked worker's hands now has soft, pink skin. The man who rose early and worked all day is now idle and lost. The man who whistled when he worked is silent. The man who said, 'I love you,' just by the look he gave, now stares blankly.

I want to know more of my father. What was he like before he came to this country? Was his character forced to change as well as his name? I want to learn about my Italian heritage, its language, its food and its traditions. I am the only daughter of six children, I love cooking, and I feel a burning need to learn all the traditions of Abruzzese cuisine. Maybe through cooking him the dishes of his childhood my dad will remember.

Winter

Cobblestone roads, *il Papa* and pepper

THE FIRST PERSON I encounter when I arrive in Italy is not my friendly and helpful cousin, Giacinto. It is Fangio. He doesn't introduce himself as Fangio but I soon discover his goal in life is to *be* Fangio. After a 28-hour journey, having survived turbulence and delays, avoided terrorist attacks and sat in airline seats designed for smaller bottoms than my own, I find myself a passenger from the airport to my hotel in the hands of Fangio. At speeds that draw my cheeks back off my face he weaves his way down freeways, busy roads and side streets to get me to Trastevere, the neighbourhood in which I have chosen to immerse myself for my week in Rome before heading to my father's village. We screech to a halt and as he deposits my luggage on the road he holds out his hand for a tip. Whether it is out of sheer relief to have my life out of his hands, the joy of starting my adventure or jetlag, I hand over far too many euros. He speeds off. Welcome to Rome.

I am dizzy at the thought of what lies ahead of me—a year with my relatives, travelling, studying Italian and immersing myself in the country and culture of Italy. I am here to live, breathe and feel Italy with all my senses. This is not my first time overseas. I have travelled a lot, lived in foreign countries for extended periods and been away from my family. But there's something different about this trip. No longer a young twenty-something in search of adventure, I'm older now, my parents are ageing and I view the world differently. I have come to realise just how precious it is to have a close, strong family around you, and how fragile.

Trastevere is everything I want it to be, a real Roman neighbourhood with a maze of tiny cobblestone streets that wind their way from A to B with everything in between. Here are streets with washing hanging out the windows, mammas calling to their children playing in the piazza below, a furniture restorer next to a blacksmith next to a bakery next to a *tobacchi*. Each day at midday I see women queuing for meat at the spotlessly clean butchers. I have never seen such pale veal. There are cheese shops with fresh ricotta in the window to entice you in; once inside, you are hit by both the aroma and the sheer variety of fresh produce on display. Busy fruit and vegetable stalls are stocked with deep-orange mandarins from Sicily, still bearing their tufts of green leaves, glistening bulbs of crisp fennel, globe artichokes plucked of their outer leaves and trimmed carefully by the shopkeeper and ready to cook, and yellow broccoli looking like a crown you can imagine the King of Thailand wearing. Everything is fresh daily. The way shopping is meant to be.

I long for a coffee but wait days until I get up the courage to actually enter a bar and order one. Ordering, drinking and partaking in coffee is such a serious ritual here that I am nervous of exposing myself as a fraud, an Italian who can't even order a coffee. Several times I stand at the door of a bar, willing myself to be brave and enter. Finally on the fifth morning I walk confidently in, order an espresso and *cornetto* from the uniformed cashier, take my receipt and stand at the bar. This first coffee, nervously sipped, surrounded by Italians on their way to work, is the best I have ever had.

Such a coffee is a normal breakfast for Italians. Their main meal is taken at lunch and usually involves several courses including *antipasto*, a collection of cured meats, preserved vegetables or *crostini* (dried breads topped with spreads or roasted vegetables); a first course, or *primo*, of pasta, soup or rice; and a main meal, called the *secondo*, of either meat or fish accompanied by a *contorno*, usually seasonal vegetables or salad. This is followed by *dolce*, a fruit or sweet dish and to finish, espresso. While this sounds like a lot of food, dinner is traditionally much lighter than lunch and Italians don't tend to snack between meals like we do. Meal times are a chance to savour and enjoy the food of the season and to spend time with family and friends. And I plan on making the most of every opportunity to do just that.

With this in mind I hunt out restaurants serving local fare to local people. I am surrounded by *pizzerie* and *trattorie*, some small and basic, some large and catering for the tourists. The latter I avoid.

Tucked in the corner of the tiny *Piazza de Renzi* in Trastevere, the small, family-run *Trattoria Da Augusto* typifies the dining experience I hope to find all over Italy. The furniture is basic, with tables covered in white paper and customers crammed in intimately. People call out '*Buon giorno*' in a familiar way as they enter and the kitchen staff responds in chorus. I watch with delight. There are no menus so the waiter slowly lists the dishes for the day. I choose *stracciatelli* soup, braised rabbit, broccoli and some red wine, while the waiter simply listens attentively. Waiters in Italy take their role seriously; I never once see one write an order down. What follows is glorious: silky egg soup, a Roman staple that warms my soul, delicate rabbit that falls off the bone and broccoli cooked to perfection and drizzled in olive oil. At the end of the meal, the waiter calculates my bill using his pen on the tablecloth—fourteen euros. I am in heaven.

Roman cuisine is particularly enticing. I revel in the local seasonal fare, consuming divine spaghetti *con cacio e pepe* (*pecorino* and pepper, with so much pepper it makes you sneeze); *a'matriciana* (which must be made with *guanciale*, cured pork cheek, never bacon or pancetta), pasta with artichokes, veal *saltimbocca* (*saltimbocca* means literally to jump in the mouth), and braised rabbit with olives. On one occasion I think I have finished a delicious oxtail ragu only to have the waitress refuse to take my plate until I have picked up the bones in my fingers and sucked them clean. I do as I am told, licking every last piece of succulence from them. The waitress then returns, and with a smile clears my place.

Pasta cacio e pepe
Pasta with cheese and black pepper

> spaghetti
> olive oil
> 1 garlic clove
> 1 handful grated *pecorino romano* cheese
> cracked pepper

Cook spaghetti in well-salted water. Just before the pasta is al dente, prepare the sauce. In a pan, gently heat a good slosh of olive oil with a whole clove of garlic. Remove the garlic and add the drained pasta, reserving some of the pasta water. Add a handful of grated *pecorino romano* cheese and lots and lots of cracked pepper. Add some pasta water to the pan and gently toss the pasta with the sauce. The cheese should go quite creamy. Don't skimp on the pepper—it's this ingredient that makes this pasta dish what it is.

I am enchanted by Rome—its chaos, its history and its boisterous personality; its mix of southern Italian attitude and northern power. It is filled with dented cars, double-parked or crammed in like sardines. I watch Romans go about their daily business in the confident manner they are famous for, always resplendent, whether a policeman in full uniform, a deli assistant in crisp, clean white or a waiter in professional white and black. And I see homeless people accompanied by large menacing-looking dogs congregate around *cucina economica*, soup kitchens run by convents.

My hotel is a converted section of one such convent and it in turn is attached to the *Chiesa San Francesco a Ripa*. It is not a big church, quite nondescript, but the bells ring several times a day and it does have an impressive sculpture by Bernini. It seems that at every corner in Rome there is a church. In the heart of Trastevere stands one of the most elegant, *Santa Maria in Trastevere*, renowned for the bright and brilliantly gold mosaics above its altar. As I sit in the piazza eating an ice-cream, I observe the Trastevere residents and tourists entering the church. Standing outside each entrance are two elderly beggars, women dressed in black with their heads covered. I can't help but smile as I watch them vie for space, with one screaming at the other for daring to come near her side of the facade. A priest comes out and speaks to them both, presumably encouraging them to either move their business elsewhere or keep it quiet. I wonder how successful their days are. I never once see anyone give them money.

From all over Rome the dome of St Peter's can be seen standing tall and proud, a constant reminder of the power and historical might of the Catholic Church. In every shop and restaurant, crucifixes hang in places of honour. Nuns in full habits, monks and priests from all corners of the world wander the streets—part tourist, part pilgrim, part loyal servant. As a lapsed Catholic, I find this all this quite intriguing. The reverence towards the Pope is in evidence as I and 200,000 others go to St Peter's Square on a Sunday to hear *il Papa* speak. I later discover this is not the usual crowd. Earlier that week there was a diplomatic row over a planned Papal visit to a university. The visit was cancelled due to student protests. The Bishop of Rome has called on all Christians to come to the square on the day of my visit as a show of defiance against the secular world and in support of the Holy Father.

The Vatican museums are extravagant and illustrate the stretch and power of the Church. After wandering though the rabbit warren of corridors, passing through the truly magnificent geography room with its ancient maps and illuminated golden ceiling, my footsteps lead to the Sistine Chapel. It's hard to appreciate the wonder of this room when I'm crammed in with hundreds of other tourists. I try to imagine it filled with cardinals contemplating their vote when a papal election is required. I have visions of all the political machinations of a parliamentary caucus meeting: alliances formed and broken, promises made and numbers counted. I stare at the ceiling and walls, carried away on waves of prattle. Every few minutes a loudspeaker breaks through the excited chatter, reminding visitors that they are in a chapel and to show respect with quiet retrospection. The room hushes, until a few brave whispers gradually grow into the chaos of a world of languages all spoken simultaneously, before being halted again by the electronic announcement. My half-hour in the chapel leaves me feeling seasick from the waves of silence to whispers to conversation to hushed silence that rolls over and over.

On previous visits to Italy I have been struck by the wonder that is the Pantheon. It is my favourite building on earth, with its facade like a worn farmer's face, scarred, pockmarked and damaged by history and its environment. A Roman temple transformed into a functioning church. As I pass through the imposing columns guarding its entrance I am struck by the sheer space that envelopes me. I return as often as I can while in Rome, passing pleasant hours sitting on the icy steps of the fountain in the centre of the piazza facing its entrance, watching people passing through its doors. One day as the skies open, I literally run to the Pantheon so I can witness the beauty of rain falling through the oculus, the hole in the ceiling. Water cascades down and bounces off the marble floor, disappearing through cleverly hidden drains; a heavenly connection between nature and man, God and the power of design.

I left Melbourne in the January summer, having experienced the hottest New Year's Eve in memory with a temperature over 45 degrees Celsius. I'd chosen New Year's Eve as my going-away celebration, melting as I cooked pasta for fifty friends and family. That heat feels far away as I stand waiting for my cousin Giacinto. I am surrounded by the sheer elegance and style of a European winter—luscious winter coats and matching fine leather boots, hats and scarves. My body, however, is rebelling after days walking the uneven surfaces of cobblestone roads. I long for the freedom of bare feet on hot sand. So far, my feet are the only part of me that feels homesick.

I am leaving Rome. Giacinto and his wife Madalena have come to take me to Capoposta, my ancestral home, a three-hour drive across the centre of Italy. As we wind our way through the mountains of Lazio and cross into Abruzzo, signs of winter are all around; trees are bare, the sky grey and the air icy cold. The closer we get to the Adriatic the more excited I become and the more thoughts of my father crowd my mind. Nearing Capoposta, I recognise the cluster of houses on the crest of the hill that is the village of his past and my mind wanders back to my first experience of Capoposta in 1993 with my brothers.

I was 23 years old, nervous and emotional. There at my eldest uncle Camillo's house, waiting to greet me, was the whole family. When the old people saw me they called me *Chiaruccia*, little Chiara, as I looked exactly like my grandmother, Nonna Chiara. I saw people who looked like my brothers. I saw my father in the faces of my cousins and my uncles. I began to connect to a people and place I had only heard about.

And with that my Italian heritage moved from the periphery to the centre of my being. I embraced having such a mixed background and became curious about my father's life. I began to ask questions and he began to tell stories.

I think back to my departure over a week ago. As I walked into my parents' house, I heard the familiar sound of Dad playing the piano accordion. He sits in the front room for a couple of hours every day, lost in his world of music. He presses the keys, pushes the base buttons and uses his arms to breathe air into the huge lungs of his red Paulo Soprani *la fisarmonica*. Joy fills his face. He often plays a wrong note and mixes tunes but they all have that familiar beat and melody of traditional Italian songs.

This instrument has become his identity, his crutch and his strength. It is his connection to his grand-children, to his past and to the world he now finds impossible to communicate in. For years Alzheimer's has slowly eaten away at his personality, his language and his capacity. It is a cruel and debilitating disease, not only for the sufferers, but those who love them. This is especially so for Mum, his companion of over fifty years.

Mum was a young 24-year-old country girl from central Victoria when she married my father. I often marvel at her courage, marrying a man from a strange faraway land who spoke little of her language and whose history and customs were so different from her own. She sits in the back room of their house, listening to my father play. It gives her a rest from looking after him and a chance to work on her favourite pastime. Her spinning wheel whirs as his accordion sings. There is calm and peace in the house.

It is my last day in Australia before I leave to spend a year in my father's homeland. I want to see what I can uncover of my father's memories, now locked away in his Alzheimer's brain. To discover the heritage and the country that has come to play such an important role in my identity and to learn the language of my father in the hope that when I return I can interpret some of what he says.

Saying goodbye is hard. I see it in my mother's eyes—her only daughter of six children leaving her. My father understands I am going to Italy but doesn't comprehend that nearly four seasons will pass before he will see his daughter again. I am excited at the prospect of having the time to completely absorb Italian life, worried that my mother feels abandoned, and fearful that Dad's condition will worsen and he will not remember me when I come home.

We drive into the village. Midday sun begins to shine and a crisp blue-sky day emerges. I hug, kiss, cry and laugh with my relatives over a meal of pasta with lamb sauce, pork cutlets from the pig slaughtered a week ago and freshly made homemade sausages.

That evening I watch through my bedroom window as the sun sets over the snow-capped Mount Maiella standing tall and gracious in front of Capoposta. Life is good.

Sugo agnello
Lamb pasta sauce

Lamb used to flavour a pasta sauce is *the* Abruzzese
sauce. If you want to make it less rich, brown the meat
separately then add to the sauce, otherwise follow
as below.

    1 onion, chopped
    1 capsicum, chopped
    1–2 garlic cloves
    olive oil
    1–2 pieces lamb (shanks, neck or good chops),
        trimmed of fat
    red wine (optional)
    2 bottles tomato pulp or 3–4 cans tomatoes,
        crushed by hand
    tied parcel of mixed herbs
    fresh basil

In a good heavy pot, gently sauté the onion,
capsicum and one or two cloves of garlic. Remove
from the pot once softened. In the same pot, heat oil
then brown the lamb. If you are feeling indulgent,
deglaze with some red wine at this point.

Return the vegetables to the pot and add the tomato
pulp and herb parcel.

Simmer covered for 1½–2 hours, by which time
there should be a generous amount of split oil
sitting on top of the sauce. Remove garlic and herbs.

Remove the meat and either serve separately or strip the bones of meat, shred it and return it to the sauce. You can add some fresh basil at this point and season just before serving.

Serve with *macheroni chitarra* (see page 38).

A note on oil: Don't be afraid of oil. There should be a generous amount glistening on the top of the sauce. Sometimes I add extra slurps while it's cooking. When you dress the pasta, use the ladle to skim the oil off the top of the sauce and toss it through the pasta before adding more sauce.

Slow days, fingerprints and *la passeggiata*

CAPOPOSTA IS A small hamlet of about twelve homes, all in a row. Some are new, some are extremely old. Some are uninhabited and others are filled with three generations living together. Every house except one is owned by a Di Sciascio, although there are two different family lines. The Di Sciascio name comes from Guardiagrele, about eight kilometres away, where the old *Palazzo Di Sciascio* still stands.

My home away from home is the house of my dad's brother, Zio Alberto, my aunt Zia Rosaria and my cousin Maria Chiara. Theirs is the family home, the house my father was born in.

I have arrived in Capoposta during slaughter season, when families kill their pig to make a year's worth of salami, sausage, cut meats for the freezer, *lonza* and prosciutto. In local dialect, this season is nicknamed *ccidere de puorci*, which literally means kill the pigs, a ruthless but accurate description. Every piece of the pig is used—either minced for salami or sausages, chopped for freezing and cooking later, or carefully selected for a specific purpose: loin for *lonza*, belly for pancetta, leg for prosciutto and so on. Even the head is not wasted. It is boiled, then the meat is scraped off and pressed into a terrine-like dish. Called *coppa*, it is eaten cold. The most crucial ingredient in all cured meats is salt, and this is calculated precisely per kilogram of meat. The choice of spices is particular to the traditions of the area and in our case, pepper, nutmeg, dried chilli, fennel and ground coriander are the essential flavours.

On my second day here I help Zia Rosaria prepare the *lonza* for curing. They killed their pig before I arrived and the *lonza* has been marinating in pepper, salt, herbs and spices for a couple of days. Our task is to pat the meat dry and wrap it in pieces of casing, tie them up tight and hang them in the attic. It is our first opportunity to work side by side and talk. She shows me what to do and even though we can't understand each other's words, her smile and her encouraging '*Brava, Angela*' let me know I'm doing OK.

Soon after, my neighbour Zia Angelina and her family invite me to their house for the day of their pig slaughter. While it is a gruesome event to bear witness to, it is also the opportunity to honour the animal that sustains them by serving a feast where pork is the central theme of the meal. Pigs are raised with care here; treated with a reverence rivalled only perhaps by their passion for olive oil. And with good reason. In times of need cured meat from the family pig was all that kept the family alive. At one point during World War II when the Allies and Germans were fighting literally on either side of Capoposta, my father's chore was to protect the prosciutto. He would take it down the valley behind the village to keep it safe, mainly from hoarding Germans who would raid the village for food. It was this meat that separated his family from those who were starving. I wonder how he felt, isolated in the valley several hundred metres below his home, clutching the prosciutto in his arms? What thoughts would have gone through his mind? Was he afraid? I will never know the answers; Alzheimer's has taken them away from me.

I arrive at Zia Angelina's to find two large dead pigs lying in the garden ready for hanging. Early that morning the men had slaughtered the animals, removed the hair, bled and gutted them. The slaughtering is a skilled if brutal undertaking, at the end of which we are left with a hairless, gutless, giant pig hanging by its feet with a large slit down its stomach. For today's feast the first cuts of meat from the belly and ribs are given to the kitchen to prepare the meal and then the pork is hung for the next three or four days before being meticulously butchered and turned into salami and other cured meats. Lunch is a highly anticipated meal that everyone is looking forward to. It is a traditional menu and very particular to the slaughter season.

Some of the pork meat is used to flavour the *sugo* for the pasta. Today Zia Angelina and her daughter-in-law Maria prepare *timballo*, which is a baked pasta dish like lasagne, but without béchamel sauce. This is followed by two main courses. The first, called *cif e ciaf*, is made of cuts of fatty, juicy pork belly, cooked in oil in an old iron pot hanging over the wood fire. This is then served with a fennel salad. In Capoposta, fennel is served sliced thick, seasoned with salt and then drizzled with olive oil and homemade wine vinegar. It is refreshing, crisp, sharp and glorious and a daily staple in winter. Sliced oranges drizzled in oil and sprinkled with cracked pepper are the perfect accompaniment. The fat of the pork belly is balanced by the acidity of the orange and the freshness of the fennel.

Next come the ribs. Roasted in a wood-fired oven with potatoes and accompanied by a green salad, they are simply heavenly. The table is silent except for the sounds of lips licking fingers. Finally there is fruit and then sweets to finish. In Abruzzo, sweets are usually small biscuits or pastries served with coffee. Dessert does not feature highly in Abruzzese cuisine; all the effort is put into the previous courses.

When my father was young, the day of the pig slaughter was a reason to celebrate. Relatives were invited and after all the work was done, a feast was shared, with a menu similar to what I experienced at Zia Angelina's. Afterwards, people would dance and sing the evening away in joyous revelry.

A few days later, I go to my cousin Nicola's house to witness the next phase of the process, salami day. When I arrive I see Nicola carrying a huge hind leg of pork on his shoulders. He smiles proudly, waves and invites me in.

Salami day is a big event involving the entire family; aunts, uncles, in-laws, and grandchildren all have a part to play. The garage has been spotlessly prepared in readiness for a production-line effort. A large table is set up in the centre and a range of knives sit sharpened, ready for use. The pig has been butchered into large pieces that are placed on the table. The most experienced workers are given the task of boning the meat, which is then passed on to the next group who cut it into small chunks ready for the mincer. Meanwhile, the liver is minced and mixed with chilli, garlic, herbs and spices to be made into liver sausages.

Nicola's mother-in-law Signora Elena, the matriarch of the family, is in charge of proceedings. She carefully selects what meat and fat will be used for what purpose. Signora Elena is gracious and calm throughout the proceedings but has no qualms about letting you know if you're not performing to her standards. I see her reject meat and return it to the production line to be cut again and expertly inspect piles of mince to ensure it has the right amount of fat.

Once the meat is minced it is weighed carefully and then spread out on the wooden table. The salt is measured precisely and sprinkled over the meat, along with peppercorns, coriander, fennel and nutmeg. All hands are involved in the massaging of the meat, with a circle of people moving around the table so the meat is mixed consistently. After this, it is put into tubs and allowed to rest.

After we break for lunch Signora Elena capably and confidently begins forming the salamis and sausages, holding the skins gently as the mince is forced through the processor. This is a delicate operation that she has been performing for her family each year for over sixty years. She generously relinquishes the processor to let me experience what making salami feels like, all the while knowing that inexperienced hands can allow too much air in or overfill the sausage, splitting the skins. She quickly takes over again when we realise just how terrible I am at it. During this process the production line continues, ends are tied, the skins pricked to release air bubbles and salamis sorted into shares for the family.

All the time people tell stories, laugh and remember. It has been a very long day, but our efforts are rewarded. We have produced hundreds of salamis and sausages, and a freezer full of meat cuts, prosciutto and *lonza*. Enough to be split between three families and last the year.

The Australian Di Sciascios have never cured our own meats but our family friends do and when they visit, bringing with them salami, my dad licks his lips in readiness and is visibly excited. I now realise it is the memory of days like this that whets his appetite; both for the flavours and the memories that they bring back.

Home-cured meats

Salt is the most crucial and carefully measured ingredient in cured meats. Generally the rule is:

> 30 g per kg of meat for *lonza*
> 25 g per kg of meat for salami (my aunt uses 23 g)
> 22 g per kg of meat for sausage (my aunt uses 20 g)

Lonza
   pork loin
   salt
   bay leaf
   rosemary
   paprika
   pepper
   white wine
   lonza casing (from your local butcher/specialist
      supplier)
   olive oil (optional)

Salt whole pork loin with the required amount of salt as per the ratios above.

In a large bowl, marinate the meat with the bay leaf, rosemary, paprika and pepper for a few days. The salt will release a pink liquid from the meat. Turn the meat three or four times a day, always leaving it in the liquid.

After three or four days, rinse the meat with white wine. Pat it dry with paper towel and wrap it in the casing. Tie tightly with string, ensuring there are no air bubbles.

Hang in a cool, dry but airy place for 3–4 months.

Serve sliced very finely.

Zia Rosaria also stores already cured *lonza* in big vats of olive oil. This makes the meat more tender and delicate than air-dried *lonza*.

Salami

  pork meat and pork fat
  salt
  black pepper
  crushed coriander seeds
  crushed fennel seeds
  nutmeg (my aunt leaves this out)
  paprika
  dried chilli powder or flakes
  sausage casings cleaned well and soaked in water
    acidulated with lemon

Mince the meat and salt with the required amount
of salt as per the ratios above. Lay the meat out
on a wood table or large chopping board. Sprinkle
with salt and pepper and massage the meat with
your hands. Let it rest a bit before adding the other
ingredients to your liking. Mix really well with your
hands then fry a small amount in a pan to taste for
seasoning. Then, use a sausage maker to squeeze into
soaked skins. Tie ends well with string and prick the
skins. Hang the salami to dry for 3–4 weeks.

Once cured, salami is best stored in vacuum-sealed
packages and kept in the fridge.

Sausage
    pork mince
    salt
    pepper
    spices as you like, but generally my relatives use
        only ground fennel and coriander or even just
        plain salt and pepper
    sausage casings

Salt the mince with the required amount of salt
as per the ratios above. Form as with salami, but
thinner. Use fresh or freeze.

My days are made up of long walks, helping my aunt
cook, visiting people and exploring the region. I help
Zia Rosaria and Zio Alberto with odd jobs around

the place, trying hard to convince my family that the tasks that seem routine to them are steeped in fascination for me.

Life is slow in the village and I gradually relax into it, but time does pass even at this languid pace and it will not be long until my tourist visa will expire. My father was naturalised as an Australian before I was born, so technically I have no right to an Italian passport, making an extended stay in Italy difficult, unless of course I can secure a *permesso di soggiorno per motivi familiari*. It took me a year to discover its existence; this permit allows those with aunts, uncles or cousins living in Italy to stay for family reasons. A *permesso*, once received, will allow me to stay with my uncle, to work, to study and to access government services. It can only be applied for after arrival in Italy.

Obtaining such a coveted document proves no mean feat. Back in Australia I had to get my birth certificate translated, notarised and stamped with an *Apostille* seal from the Department of Foreign Affairs and Trade and then present said documents to the Italian Consulate for stamping and pay a nominal tax.

Armed with the appropriate paperwork and evidence from the local municipality testifying to the link between my father and Zio Alberto, Maria Chiara and I head off to the immigration office in the provincial capital, Chieti.

At the immigration office I experience Italy in all its bureaucratic splendour. I bounce endlessly back and forth securing more tax stamps, extra photos and additional documentation only to discover that the biggest hold-up is my hands. I am fingerprinted twice, once by the immigration officer and once by the police. Both times my hands fail to create fingerprints on the digital scanner. Apparently I have very fine prints. By law, they must have three attempts at using the computer scanner before resorting to the old-fashioned ink pad method. I have to return in two weeks to try again before they will process my papers. In the intervening time my aunt becomes very protective of my hands, making sure I use gloves and hand cream in an attempt to reveal my bashful prints. On a Saturday I go to the local police station to be interviewed so they can confirm I am a genuine case and that I really am staying at my uncle's house.

As I weave my way through this administrative labyrinth I think about the preparations my father made for his journey to Australia. The certificate of good character he had to obtain, the medical examinations he had to endure and the interviews conducted by Australian officials that must have seemed so foreign and strange. My frustrations pale in comparison.

After a couple of weeks in Capoposta I pluck up the courage to drive my uncle's old Fiat Panda into the main town of Casoli, eight kilometres away from home. I am timid at best, not only because I am driving on the opposite side along very narrow, hilly and windy roads, but also because everyone here drives a manual.

It's been a long time since I've driven a manual, not to mention one with the gears on the wrong side. Somehow I survive and find myself in Casoli, a beautiful village of narrow, winding streets perched atop a steep hill. I drive around town several times in search of a car park that doesn't require parallel parking.

The Abruzzo countryside has seduced me into going for long walks every day. I rug up in my winter clothes and head out into the crisp, chilly mountain air. This creates much conversation in Capoposta and surrounding villages. Apparently it is quite strange to see people walking between villages at all, let alone in the depths of winter. Word has spread and my uncle has been answering lots of questions about the 'girl walking along the road'. He tells them who I am and why I am here in the hope they might wave instead of simply staring. For me the walking has become a necessity, not only for my soul but also to avoid an ever-expanding girth as a result of Zia Rosaria's fine cooking.

Walking is the perfect way to appreciate the idyll that is Capoposta. I watch people going about their business—families pruning olives, old ladies toiling in their gardens and farmers ploughing their fields. All the time the imposing Mount Maiella watches over me, the tranquillity broken only by the furious barking of village dogs tied to posts, and worse still the yapping and nipping at my ankles by those left to run loose.

When I was a child, my dad never allowed us to have a pet dog. He insisted that a suburban house was no place to keep a dog, that dogs needed wide open spaces and fresh air. As a result, I never got used to being around them and perhaps that's where my fear stems from. Then again, maybe it's one that I've inherited. When my dad was young it wasn't just dogs he had to be wary of, but mountain wolves. In times of hunger they would venture down from the mountain to hunt for food around the homes and farms of the valley. If they were really hungry, they would attack humans. Today wolves are rarely if ever seen in this part of Italy.

The season is slowly hinting at change. The snow has gone from our village now, residing only on the highest mountain tops. The ground is becoming greener as small shoots start pushing their way through, and the farmers are ploughing the fields in readiness for milder temperatures. I watch them pruning their olive trees and grape vines. Everything is coming to life again, including my aunt's vegie patch, which is filled with greens bursting with healthy promise. The sky is blue now, but the air is still crisp and cold. The sun is warm on my back as I walk. I hear birds and, at all hours of the day, roosters crowing. I cannot wait for spring.

Verdura
Mixed greens

This is delicious as a side dish or you could add pasta for a winter meal. My grandmother would make this dish. She would add pieces of rustic corn bread, cover the pan with a lid, cover the lid with coals and cook it on the floor of a wood fire—in dialect this is called *pizz e foie*.

> mixed greens, such as *rapa*, broccolini, cabbage, silverbeet, Tuscan cabbage and chicory etc.
> ⅓ cup good olive oil
> 1 garlic clove, smashed
> dried capsicum skins or paprika
> dried chilli, optional

Parboil mixed greens. Add to a pan and heat gently.

In a separate pan, heat the olive oil with a smashed garlic clove. Let the garlic infuse then remove. Add a good teaspoon of homemade dried capsicum skins (or good paprika), and some chilli flakes if you like. Pour the hot oil over the greens and toss well while heating. Serve.

Variation: Add potato pieces at the parboiling stage. They should be well cooked.

The Di Sciascios of Capoposta are known by their nickname *i paiari*, which in dialect means a small structure made of wood, reeds and straw. Legend has it that my great, great grandfather Mattia was the first Di Sciascio to settle in Capoposta. At that time there were no houses here and he lived very simply, perhaps in a straw house. Eventually he married, established a small farm, built a house and adopted his nephew, my great grandfather Domenico, who went on to have seven children, one of whom was my grandfather, Nonno Mattia. The name Mattia is an important one in our family. In Abruzzo, the tradition is to name your first son after the paternal grandfather. My eldest brother is Matthew, my grandfather is Mattia and his grandfather was called Mattia. All through my Italian family, the same male names keep appearing: Mattia, Domenico, Nicola, Camillo, Brescio and Giuseppe. History repeating, ancestors remembered, traditions kept.

When my father was young, Capoposta was a busy place filled with families. There were the Di Sciascios who worked their own land and there was a group of families who worked on a large property owned by a wealthy doctor. These families were the unfortunate ones, labouring under a feudal system that was harsh and desperate. Every day on my walks I pass this property, called *il casino* by locals. The families who lived here then were trapped in a life of poverty in order to feed a distant master. The collection of buildings, including an old chapel, stand deserted now, long abandoned. The doctor's descendant, Don Franco, still visits daily, but now he grows his own vegetables and crops and is a much-loved member of the small Capoposta community.

Capoposta is on a rise between two valleys. Sloping down the valleys is a patchwork of fields belonging to various members of our and neighbouring villages.

There are no large allotments of land here, only small plots, passed down from fathers to sons, the patchwork a testament to land split and shared. Some have olives, some are for vines, some for vegetables and the rest for crops. I am amazed watching the tractors negotiate such steep terrain.

Farms here don't just produce crops though. Milk, veal and lamb are staple produce of the local farms. Unlike in Australia, farmers here don't graze their animals. Pigs, cattle and sheep are kept in stables and meticulously cared for. There are chickens and rabbits too. One day I accompany Zia Rosaria and my cousin Mattia's wife Silvana to buy a fresh batch of baby rabbits for rearing. We arrive at the local agricultural suppliers early so they can be first in line to pick the healthiest looking bunnies. As we wait, more and more women arrive to collect their order. A truck pulls up, loaded with dozens of small crates packed high inside larger ones. Inside each small crate are at least ten rabbits. Zia collects her seven and Silvana her eleven, inspecting each carefully and rejecting any that don't fit their criteria. The vendor lifts the rabbits individually by the scruff of the neck and counts aloud, ensuring both vendor and buyer agree on the number.

The drive home is gentle, conscious of the precious cargo on board, but still the rabbits scratch and screech until they are let loose in the freshly prepared pen where they will live happy and comfortable lives until it comes time for them to feed our family.

Zio Alberto is seventy-five now, so he only has four cows, twenty-one chickens, a pig, and about a dozen rabbits at various ages. Life is simple but still hard. His stable is small and is the original stable of my father's childhood. His cousin next door has a large purpose-built stable that houses over twenty cows. Their care requires hours of backbreaking work. Land is both precious and scarce here and every inch needs to be used effectively to sustain a family.

My aunt has two kitchens. This at first seems extravagant to me. One is beautiful and newly reno-vated and, like in all Italian homes, is the heart of the house. The TV sits in the corner and it is around the dining table that most conversations, entertaining and deliberations occur. In this kitchen, my aunt bakes cakes and boils pasta. Her pride and joy, however, is the second kitchen, in the shed next to the stable. This shed has an open fire, a big new wood oven, another stove, a pasta-making table, a sink, a spare fridge and a variety of other mysterious equipment. The most important dishes are prepared here: the fresh pasta, the stock, the sweets. It is here that vegetables are preserved and animals butchered, roasted and barbecued over hot coals. The pasta table belonged to Nonna Chiara, and is very old. Its top is worn from years of kneading. It is a table that has fed several generations.

Most afternoons I spend sitting in front of the fire in the shed watching my aunt and uncle go about their business in and out of the stable next door. On

Saturdays I often help my aunt make pasta here and on Sundays she might cook a six-course family meal in the wood oven. If the kitchen is the heart of the house, the shed is the lifeblood of the family.

Chitarra is the traditional shape of pasta for Abruzzo. *Chitarra* (pronounced kitarra) is also the name of the pasta-cutting equipment used in Abruzzo. A *chitarra* is a true Abruzzese tradition and in essence looks like a guitar—tight metal strings tied onto a wooden frame. You roll the pasta dough over the strings, which cut the pasta into a square spaghetti-like shape. The cut strips of pasta are caught below in a wooden 'catcher'. *Chitarra* is my favourite shape of pasta and it is quite easy to use the *chitarra* rack rather than a pasta machine. You can buy a *chitarra* in specialist Italian importers, but they are quite expensive. I carried one home all the way from Italy, purchased from an old man who hand-made it in his village, high in the Abruzzo mountains.

Nearly every recipe book I own says to use '00' grade flour for pasta making. In Italy, flour is graded by how finely it is milled, 00 being the most refined. Flour can also be made of two types of grain, hard wheat and soft wheat; most 00 flour is made from soft wheat flour. Every person I ask in Abruzzo says that 00 flour is for sweets and pastries and that you must use hard wheat flour (durum wheat) for pasta. The further south in Italy you travel, the harder the wheat and the fewer the eggs are used in pasta. In Australia, if you use 00, the pasta does have a different consistency on your palate and is much easier to handle. Most Australian Abruzzese I know use a mixture of 00 flour and *grana dura di semola*, semolina flour. It is now quite easy to find flour labelled specifically for pasta in Australian supermarkets and delis. If you use a *chitarra*, the pasta dough needs to be quite hard, as the softer the flour, the more it sticks to the wires. Pasta made with soft flour and eggs is good for delicate filled pastas like tortellini or ravioli.

Macheroni Chitarra

> 200 g flour
> 2 eggs
> pinch of salt
> tepid water
> a little semolina for dusting

Place the flour on a large pasta board and make a well. Place the eggs in the well and add a pinch of salt. Have some tepid water on hand in case needed. Using 100 g of flour with one egg will make enough for an entrée serve for two people, so this recipe should produce enough for four.

With the tips of your fingers, gently mix the eggs and gradually incorporate some of the flour. Keep incorporating until the dough is dry enough to start kneading. Kneading pasta takes time and effort. Keep kneading until the flour is fully combined.

If necessary, add a little tepid water but be very careful not to add too much. As you knead, scrape and gather any stray bits that don't absorb into the ball and add to the middle of the dough. Use flour to clean your hands of any sticky bits and incorporate them into the dough too. Keep kneading until fully combined and the board is clean. Cover the pasta dough with a bowl, plastic wrap or a tea towel and let rest for about 10 minutes.

When you return to the kneading, rub a little oil on your hands. Keep kneading until the dough is as smooth as a baby's bottom. It should have no flecks of flour and have a consistent texture. This should take about 8 minutes of kneading. My aunt kneads lengthways. That is, she uses her body to form a long horizontal bread loaf shape a bit like a baguette. Then she doubles it over and kneads again. She ends up with a long piece of dough that looks like a log. I prefer to knead it into a round shape.

Cut a piece the size of your palm and thickness of your hand from the rested dough. With your hand, gently stretch the piece so it can be placed into the pasta machine. Pass the piece through at setting number 1 (the widest setting) four times, each time folding the piece three times. Then go to number 3 and pass through once, then once at 4 and twice at 5.

Cut the pasta into strips the size of the *chitarra*. Place a strip on the *chitarra* and use the short rolling pin to roll away from your body gently, but with pressure. Then gently roll back and forth until the pasta is cut by the *chitarra* strings. Don't worry if there is pasta left at the top. Flip it over back towards you and use the pin to cut with the *chitarra*. If any pasta gets stuck on the *chitarra*, gently strum the strings and the pasta will release. Continue in this way with the rest of the pasta dough. If you don't have a *chitarra*, use the *tagliatelle* cutting tool on a pasta machine.

Place pasta on cardboard trays and dust with semolina so it doesn't stick. Freeze on the trays or keep covered with a tea towel in a cool dry place and serve later that day.

Cooking pasta can feel like a science. When boiling homemade pasta, use a large pot filled with lots of water. Salt the water well. Add some oil to prevent sticking. Never add oil to packet pasta—it is not necessary. Be careful to watch the pasta while it is cooking as the flour can react to the water and rise aggressively in a froth and overflow the pot. This can be dangerous so try not to include all the flour from the pasta tray when adding the pasta to the water. Don't overfill the water and be ready to turn down the heat if you see the froth rising. Remember to stir gently using a wooden pasta fork.

Homemade pasta is more filling than dried pasta, especially if it is made with eggs. Fresh pasta can be heavy in your stomach if not cooked long enough so I always cook fresh pasta to a less al dente point than dried pasta for this reason. That is, it is a little more well-done than dried pasta. When cooked, add cold water to the pot to stop the cooking process and drain ready for serving. You will need a generous amount of sauce with homemade pasta. Always toss the sauce through the pasta before serving. In Italy I have never seen pasta served undressed with a spoon of sauce on top as I have seen in Australia—it defeats the whole purpose of marrying the pasta shape and texture to the sauce.

A pasta board should be at least 2½ cm thick, and be 95 cm wide and 65 cm deep. Along one of the long sides there needs to be a lip so that it fits flush against the side of the table as you put a lot of body pressure onto the board when kneading. This lip will prevent the board from slipping.

Pizzocheri is perhaps one of the most interesting pasta dishes I have tasted in Italy. Originating from the Lombardy mountains, it has buckwheat flour as the main ingredient. It is an incredibly rich and heavy winter dish and perfectly suited to the ruggedness of the weather. I first had this many years ago in Galway, Ireland at my friend Giuliana's house. She had just come back from Lombardy and brought with her a packet of *pizzocheri*, which her sons were very excited about. Strangely enough, the cabbage, potato and buckwheat pasta seemed to suit the Irish environment just as well.

Pizzocheri

500 g dried *pizzocheri* or make your own following
    the directions below
300 g cabbage, chopped
300 g potatoes, chopped into cubes
sage
4 garlic cloves
250 g butter
150 g parmesan, grated
500 g *fontina* cheese, chopped into small pieces
extra butter for serving

For the pasta

250 g buckwheat flour
100 g plain flour
2 eggs
4 tbsp milk
pinch of salt

If making the pasta by hand, combine the flours and place on a pasta board, making a well in the middle. Add the eggs, milk, salt and some water if needed to make the dough. Knead until smooth and elastic, which will take about 10 minutes. Rest the dough for 30 minutes. Use a pasta machine to roll 5 mm sheets, then cut the sheets into strips the length and width of your index finger.

In a large pot, boil dried pasta, cabbage and potato in lots of water. If using fresh pasta, add to the pot after the vegetables are almost tender.

Meanwhile, brown the sage and garlic in butter. When the pasta is ready, drain the pasta, potatoes and cabbage into a large heated serving bowl. Add some of the parmesan, *fontina* cheese and butter and stir. Keep adding gradually until all is used.

This dish should be rich, heavy and sticky. The potatoes should melt in your mouth. It is quite amazing what the sage brings to this dish.

I am in the shed sitting in front of the fire when a strange thing happens. I hear a whistle. It is the whistle Dad makes as he walks up the side of my house to visit me. It is his 'I am here' whistle and for an instant I think it is my dad outside the door. I go out to see who is there. It's our neighbour, Dad's cousin Biasetto, announcing his entry to the stable where my uncle and aunt are milking the cows. I am comforted by the familiarity of the whistle. It reminds me of my dad. It connects me to Capoposta.

Every evening Zio Alberto asks me questions about life in Australia and about his brother, my dad. He likes to hear about our daily lives and comparisons to Italy, and I in turn yearn to hear stories of their childhood. When we were children Dad did speak of Italy but not often. We were more connected to my mother's side of the family with endless aunts, uncles and cousins, and holidays at Grandma's farm. It was hard for us to relate to a place we had never seen, people we had never met and traditions we seldom practised. Now I am making up for lost time. My Italian family has become accustomed to me sitting with my notebook madly scribbling down everything my uncle says. He is Dad's last surviving sibling and I feel duty-bound to gather as many stories as I can. I ache to capture the essence of their life here for my nieces, for my siblings, for me, and as a tribute to my father and the life he left behind.

But life has changed much here since my father's time. When he and my uncle were younger they fetched water from distant wells, they had no electricity, and they hung out in the stable with cows to keep warm on winter nights. There was handmade pasta every day in times of plenty, shared in a house that was home to two or three families. There were no cars and they farmed by hand. Now I sit in my room with my laptop connected to the internet via my mobile phone and we watch satellite TV every night.

Most days I visit someone from the village, often accompanied by my cousin Domenichella. She doesn't speak English but has a wonderful way of translating dialect into very simple Italian that I can usually comprehend. We are an enterprising couple, visiting old people who talk non-stop to me, despite each of us not understanding a thing the other says. But our hosts are content simply to see me and to recognise my father in my face.

I go with my aunt to visit my cousin Antonietta. She is my oldest cousin and well over sixty. It is strange having a cousin who is as old as an aunt, but she is the daughter of Dad's eldest sister, Carmella, who was married and had children before my father left for Australia. Antonietta's face shines with happiness when she sees me. She has an all-embracing way of saying hello. Her strong arms hold me tight and she smothers me with kisses. Tears well in her eyes and despite our lack of a common language I am transported back to my childhood by her embrace, an embrace so reminiscent of the greetings of our dear family friend Felicetta.

Saturday evenings my cousin Maria Chiara and I often go to Lanciano, about twenty minutes away by car. Saturday night is a sight to behold in Lanciano. The main street is closed to traffic and full of people of all ages doing *la passeggiata*, the slow walk. Dressed in their finest, they parade up and down the street, saying hello to everyone and checking everyone out. By 9.30 pm the streets are silent as everyone packs into the many *pizzerie*. Later again out everyone comes, parading once more. I've been to Italy several times and I'm always astounded at this ritual that occurs in towns and cities all over the country, especially the south. It is both lovely and strange seeing all ages out enjoying time together.

Back in Australia I am an English language teacher. It is a rewarding career and perhaps a choice nourished by a deep-seated desire to understand my father's migrant experience. As I teach I witness his challenges through the experiences of my students. Now in Italy I find the shoe is firmly on the other foot. My Italian is slowly improving and I understand a lot more than when I first came. I comprehend more than I can speak, although my aunt is easier to understand than my uncle. Maria Chiara's English is excellent but while she is at work it's just me and Zio and Zia. I get extremely tired and after a while I simply have to close my mind and escape.

Historically, Italy was made of a hundreds of city states, each with its own language. Standard Italian as we know it is quite a modern phenomenon, spreading across Italy in recent centuries largely due to the publication of two iconic Italian works of literature, Dante Alighieri's *Divine Comedy* and *The Betrothed* by Alessandro Manzoni. Even though Italy is a modern country, regional, provincial and municipal dialects are still commonplace. Standard Italian is taught at school and used professionally but often the local dialect is still spoken at home.

Capoposta is on the edge of two dialects—Casolani and Guardiagrele. My dad's family speaks Casolani but some of his in-laws came from villages that spoke the

Guardiagrele dialect. Speakers of the two dialects can understand each other but every day I am astounded at just how different they are from each other and from standard Italian. Zio Alberto recalls that when Dad would visit they noticed that he had lost some of his dialect as a result of mixing with Italians from all over Italy in Australia. But with the advancement of Alzheimer's Dad has reverted to his native tongue. For his children who only know a little standard Italian, and even my mum who knows a lot of standard Italian, this is challenging.

With the changing of the seasons comes Carnevale, a festival signifying the beginning of Lent, the Catholic fasting period leading up to Easter. It's a time of celebration, indulgence and irreverence, where people poke fun at themselves and their political leaders. As with many festivals in Italy, there are age-old traditions that go with it.

In Casoli, there is a folk band that forms just for the Carnevale parade. The performers wear bright red costumes with plastic buttocks attached to their behinds and play instruments made from household objects—coffee pots for cymbals, giant wooden pasta forks, makeshift toilets for drums, and guitars made out of oven racks. Large floats portray Italian and world leaders in comical ways; one has Silvio Berlusconi dancing with Prodi, the opposition leader, and another features a giant topless Carla Bruni, the Italian wife of the French President. Children dressed as princesses, superheroes, hobos and skeletons march up and down the street excitedly, spraying each other and onlookers with foam. Amongst them are my cousin Antonio's children Elio and Mario.

There are special cakes just for Carnevale and I help my aunt make one of them, *cicerchiata*, a traditional Abruzzese Carnevale sweet. *Cicerchiata* is made up of small fried pastry balls fashioned like *cicerchie*, an ancient legume shaped like a chickpea. The pastry balls are blended with hot honey, cinnamon and almonds and formed into a wreath-like ring. After setting, it is cut into slices and served at the end of a Carnevale meal. The preparation takes hours and is incredibly detailed, leaving me both envious of Italy's long history and the enticing dishes that have been created to accompany events upon the calendar, and exhausted at the prospect of making them all.

Cicerchiata
Abruzzese Carnevale festival cake

> 5 eggs
> 60 g caster sugar
> 100 ml olive oil
> 500 g plain flour (or enough for the wet ingredients)
> sunflower oil for frying

350 g honey
2 tsp cinnamon (approx)
100 g roasted slivered almonds (approx)

Mix the eggs, sugar and olive oil. Put the flour
on a pasta board and make a well. Put the wet
ingredients into the well and using a fork gradually
incorporate the flour as you would if making pasta.
Make a dough and knead well for 4–5 minutes.
Wrap in cling wrap and let rest for 30 minutes
in the fridge. When ready, take pieces of dough
and roll with your hands into long worms about
½–1 cm thick. Cut into small pieces the size of a
chickpea. Fry in sunflower oil in batches.

To drain the pastry, place an upturned pasta plate in
the bottom of a large bowl and cover with kitchen
towel, so that when you put the pastry balls in the
bowl the oil drains and doesn't soak the pastry.

Melt honey and boil until it is a syrupy consistency.
Put the fried pastry in a large bowl and mix with
the cinnamon and roasted slivered almonds, then
add the honey mixture. Stir so that all the pastry
is coated with the honey, working quickly, as the
honey gets very sticky as it cools. Form the pastry
balls into a ring shape on a serving dish. Refrigerate
overnight. Slice and serve.

Cold days, cooking schools and heroes

WINTER IS CERTAINLY still upon us and the icy wind cuts me to the bone. Every day we watch the weather forecast as delivered by air-force colonels; Abruzzo, especially its capital L'Aquila, seems the coldest place in Italy. People here survive by wearing fur coats or knee-length puff jackets filled with down. I see so many beautiful ladies out shopping in their elegant fur coats, hair fully coiffed, gold jewellery and lipstick.

Eventually the weather catches up with me and I spend two days in bed with a shocking head cold and fever. Zia Rosaria is a very good nurse, squeezing oranges and making fresh chicken soup. As my appetite returns I decide to try an Australian cure-all for breakfast. For all my worshipping of traditional Italian cooking it is Vegemite squeezed onto toast from my one travel tube, carefully rationed, that proves my ultimate cure. The worst has passed, but my illness leaves me feeling a little homesick and I spend one and a half hours on the phone to Mum and Dad, even having a short conversation with Dad in his own language, putting a bounce back in my step.

Compared to the Monday to Friday routine of those back home, people here seem to work odd hours. Italians only work thirty-six hours a week. Some work six hours a day, six days a week. Others, like Maria Chiara, work from eight in the morning to two in the afternoon three days a week and to six in the evening two days a week. For me this is perfect, as it means we have three afternoons a week as well as weekends to go out and do things. We get in the car and head off to various places around Abruzzo, exploring all over Chieti province.

We have done lots of travelling along the coastline. Abruzzo is famous for *trabocchi*, giant wooden fishing platforms with a net and pulley system. Looking like they would be more at home in Asia than western Europe, they closely resemble enormous seaside insects with their wooden claws that stretch out to the sea. The fact that they are wood and not stone adds to their mystique, as timber is noticeably absent from most

Abruzzo architecture. Yet this ancient form of fishing is unique to the region and in particular the coast south of Pescara, where they are still in use today.

I am a little concerned the freshness and quality of Abruzzese seafood will be wasted on me as I'm not much of a sea creature eater. Even so, I find myself in a beautifully picturesque restaurant near the seaside city of Vasto, literally on the water's edge amongst the old remains of a *trabocco* in the water.

The menu we eat our way through is long and begins with an *antipasto* of cold and hot seafood dishes of chilled marinated octopus, fresh sardines cured in vinegar, and calamari in a vinegary sauce, as well as prawns seared in their shell, a bowl of mussels and clams steamed in wine, and calamari cooked in a spicy sauce. For the *primo* plate we are served ravioli filled with prawn meat accompanied by a tomato and cream sauce, and fresh *chitara* spaghetti with a mixture of shellfish with olive oil. My *secondo* is a mixed grill of seafood including filleted fish, calamari and prawns. My cousin has *frittura mista;* mixed seafood lightly deep-fried. It is surely the most seafood I have eaten in almost ten years and surprisingly I enjoy the regional quality and variety of the dishes almost as much as the spectacular view.

I love to cook. This is handy as I also love to eat. An important part of my itinerary therefore is a visit to Villa Santa Maria. This village is in the Sangro River valley in Abruzzo and is built out of the rock cliffs on the edge of a mountain. It is particularly famous for its cooking school, the oldest in Italy, founded in 1560. In Italy, when you turn fourteen or fifteen, you select what type of school you will go to—either a school for preparation for university or a professional/ vocational school. If you choose a vocational school, you go to the school in your province for that vocation. Many famous chefs have been trained at the Villa Santa Maria hospitality school.

We arrive mid-afternoon and Maria Chiara and I ask if we can have a look around. Because I am *stranieri*, a foreigner, we are instead treated to an escorted tour of the facility. I feel privileged as our guide, one of the teachers, explains the cooking equipment and how the program is run. After the tour, we walk around the town, a town dedicated to chefs. Saint Francis Caracciolo, who was born in Villa Santa Maria, is the patron saint of all Italian cooks and in October every year the *Festa dei Cuochi*, the festival of cooks, is held here. For three days chefs come from afar and students from the cooking school join together to parade, cook and display their magical creations to the public.

Despite its long history, Italian cuisine is distinctive in its simplicity, a simplicity often born of necessity, of *cucina povera*, the food of peasants. Some of the most delicate pasta sauces you can taste in Italy only consist of a few ingredients.

Zucchini and carrot pasta

1 ripe tomato, peeled and chopped
farfelle or *fussili* pasta
1 small red onion, finely chopped
1 carrot, grated
1 zucchini, grated
1 garlic clove, smashed
olive oil
cracked pepper and salt
basil leaves

To peel the tomato, cut a small cross at the base and place in boiling water for a minute. Remove and place in ice-cold water. The skin should then be easily removed.

Cook *farfelle* or *fussili* pasta in lots of salted water. In a pan, gently sauté the onion, carrot, zucchini and garlic in enough oil so that the pasta can be coated with oil. Add the chopped tomato and season Drain the pasta and toss through the sauce. Remove the garlic and garnish with whole basil leaves.

I am in love with the social life of Abruzzo. From small gatherings of friends in a *pizzeria* to late nights out dancing at a nightclub, there is always a buzz in the air, people deeply engaged in conversation. Socialising in Italy is just that—socialising. There is no need for the distraction of alcohol. Friends talk, talk and talk. I spend a few very social days in Pescara visiting my friend Enza whom I met while she was an English student at my TAFE Institute. She is a perfect illustration of the social Italian. I have never known anyone to have so many friends, to be able to talk all day, with anyone about anything, and to truly embrace life.

Pescara is a new city, developed after World War I from a small fishing village to become the industrial capital of Abruzzo. It looks and feels a bit like Geelong and is a surprisingly nice change from the hilltop towns with narrow winding streets that I've become accustomed to.

Enza is a cooking teacher at the hospitality school in Pescara. It is equivalent to the one in Villa Santa Maria and has twelve hundred students. I decide to sit in on one of her classes before having a look around the school. The facilities are very old and they are currently begging the local government to build them a new school. For all our differences it seems local governments are the same the world over.

The class I sit in on is taking its mid-term theory test and as Enza and I quietly chat at the front of the class I spot the usual cheating and sharing of answers. At one stage Enza leaves the room and instantly all the students are up comparing answers. Later I laugh as I tell her who the worst offenders were. She says she knows; 'Those boys think I don't but I do.' Perhaps students and teachers the world over are not so different either.

After school we go shopping at Pescara's only Chinese supermarket, tucked away behind the train station. I help her buy ingredients for an Asian cooking day for her students. She was inspired in Australia to cook Asian. I sound like an expert, which I am not, but at least I know what the ingredients can be used for. We practise on Monday night, making spring rolls that are well received by our guinea pig dinner guests.

Italians are far from adventurous when it comes to their food. In Italy you can find Italian restaurants, and that's just about all. There is a smattering of other cuisines dotted here and there, but nothing like the world at our doorstep that populates most Australian high streets. While I adore Italian food, I find myself craving a Thai laksa, an Indian curry, a Vietnamese pho or a Chinese fried rice. I wonder how Dad coped in Australia without his native food every day. What did he crave?

As Dad's ability to communicate has become more difficult, one way he expresses his emotions is by refusing food. He will go through periods of not eating green beans, or rice, or some other basic ingredient. When he is really upset he can refuse to eat anything. Mum tries to entice him with his favourites—pasta, chicken wings or roast potatoes—but often even this doesn't work. One dish that does always put a smile on his face is ice-cream. But man cannot live on ice-cream alone. The stress this causes Mum is palpable, exacerbated by the fact that we often don't know what it is that has made my father upset. If only he could tell us what he is feeling.

Together with my cousin Antonio and his young family, I spend a relaxing Sunday in Ortona, a very old port town not far from my village. Ortona is a lovely city with the most spectacular promenade above the sea. The promenade ends at a castle that was built in the 1450s to protect Ortona from the then enemy, the Venetians. Today it is a beautiful light-tan stone structure that juts spectacularly out into the ocean. Ortona was also an important front in World War II and there is a British cemetery nearby. I recently came across images of the Battle of Ortona in a book that showed distraught families, streets turned to rubble, hungry and desperate people carrying possessions on their heads, and the darkness of destruction on every page. The devastation was unbelievable.

War had a lasting effect on my father's family. My grandfather's dreams of buying large parcels of land around Capoposta were cut short by World War I. He and his brothers were in America working to save money when the Italian government ordered all the diaspora to return to fight or risk never being allowed back to Italy. My Nonno lost three siblings to that war.

On 1 September 1939, the war in Europe was announced with the blast of a loud siren from Guardiagrele. The sound rang out across the whole valley, heralding the start of a period of hunger, fear, terror and chaos for the people of Capoposta that would last for many years. At one point the Capoposta residents were caught between the Americans in the village next to them and the Germans who were in Guardiagrele about eight kilometres away. For about six months fighting was going on all around them, peppered with alternating visits from intimidating Germans during the day and polite Americans at night.

One morning my father's family woke to discover that approximately sixty Germans had stationed themselves in Capoposta and that my father's cousin's house had been commandeered by German officers. Zio Alberto tells me the unwanted guests weren't too bad and often played with the children. He remembers playing with one soldier called Alberto, the same as him. Another spoke politely to Nonna Chiara, calling her mamma. He showed her photos of his family who had all died. He told her that one day he would kill himself as he had no reason to live. For all their pleasantries, however, the Germans quickly ate the village out of all its food stocks, including the forty chickens they relied on for eggs.

As my grandfather had lived in America for some time before World War I he was often called upon by the Americans as a translator, putting his family at great risk. Once he helped four escaped American prisoners of war. Zio Alberto recalls one of them as being a very tall man who was very grateful for the help given to him. When he departed he scribbled his name and address on a tiny piece of paper and told my grandfather to contact him if he ever needed anything. Fearful that the note would be discovered by the Germans it was burned in the kitchen fire. To this day my uncle wonders as to the fate of the tall American and what became of his life.

Those six months must have been terrifying and very hungry times for the people of Capoposta. Near the end of the war as the Germans were retreating, people feared for their lives. Many left to find refuge. For nearly two days old people, children and animals trudged along in wintery conditions. Dad was seventeen years old at the time.

One day while finding shelter in a village he went to the *cantina* to get wine with some other children. As they were walking out of the *cantina* he saw a plane sweep overhead, its machine gun rat-a-tat-tatting down towards the ground. My father swept the children back into the *cantina* but he was still exposed and his leg was shot. Today one of the boys he saved lives on the road into Casoli. A couple of years ago he came to Australia and visited my dad. These are the experiences that helped make my father who he is today. Experiences he now can't recall. Experiences I must capture.

The end of war didn't mark the end of hardship or indeed terror. The surrounding fields were littered with land mines, discarded weapons and debris and there was a period of lawlessness as things settled back down after occupation. Without telling his parents, my dad bought himself a pistol on the black market and carried it with him for protection. One day as he was cleaning it he shot himself in the finger. Unable to reveal to his parents what he had done, he just had to live with the injury. Years later he complained of a sore finger. His best friend accompanied him to the hospital where an x-ray revealed a bullet fragment lodged in the bone.

I've kept up my daily walks around Capoposta and now people wave to me. Farmers in tractors pass me by, raising their hands in greeting. Old women dressed in dark clothes, head scarves and aprons wish me '*buon viaggio*', equivalent to 'good journey'. I am forever seeing these women toiling in their vegie patches, tying bundles of firewood or caring for their chickens, rabbits and other kitchen animals. One day an old man working in his garden looks at me. I've noticed him before. I call out good morning and he waves me over. I greet him in my best Italian, '*Buon giorno. Mi chiamo Angela Di Sciascio, figlia di Valentino Di Sciascio in Australia.*' 'Hello, my name is Angela and I am the daughter of Valentino in Australia.' He looks at me for a moment and then registers who I am. He seems very pleased and we manage to have a good ten minute chat, most of which I don't understand.

When I get home I tell my uncle all about him and he fills me in on this friendly near 90-year-old man called Giuseppe who was a friend of my dad's. He spoke English as a younger man and even gave some lessons to my dad and his friend Silvino before their journey to Australia in 1952. I am now bound to stop at his house next time for a coffee and biscuit. I have no idea what we'll talk about or how, but it is nice just being there.

It has been one month since I arrived in Capoposta. Next Friday I head off on the next leg of my grand tour—Florence. I have enrolled in a language school and can't wait to start.

Spring

Back to school
and gelato

I'VE NEVER BEEN to Florence before so this is
an especially exciting treat for me. Bursting with
art, architecture, history, culture, marble, cobblestone roads, gelato shops, well-dressed ladies, proud
Florentines, and of course, thousands of tourists,
Florence is a living, breathing gallery of Italian life.

Maria Chiara accompanies me to Florence and
we spend a lovely weekend together. We dine at cosy
restaurants, have a glass of bubbly *prosecco* in the
piazza, shop, visit the great Uffizi and shake hands with
Michelangelo's David at the Galleria Accademia. David
is breathtaking. We also indulge in far too many gelati
but they are so incredibly creamy and displayed so
beautifully—literally enticing us to eat them endlessly.

My accommodation has been arranged by the language school. I have a room in an apartment in the centre of town near the central market. The room is rented from a middle-aged school teacher who speaks no English. His apartment is typically Italian—grand wooden doors on the street open onto a narrow, steep, musty and poky concrete staircase leading to two apartments in the building. His is on the top floor but thankfully he helps me carry my luggage up the stairs. The apartment is small but cosy. The walls are covered in art and the floors with an array of Persian rugs. It's my kind of place.

I finally have a kitchen to myself so I stock up at the supermarket and cook the first meal I've made for myself in about seven weeks. I have a TV and a bathroom so I am lucky as I won't have to share these with my landlord. The bathroom is tiny and it's a bit of a logistical exercise for me not to spray water absolutely everywhere but I soon learn to make sure the toilet paper is out of the bathroom before I shower. I have a desk and a wardrobe and a double bed. The only downside is that my landlord has an unpleasant habit of touching me inappropriately as he talks. I report this to my language school and I'm given the option to move. I decide to stay. The location is so perfect.

Florence is compact and flat, so it's easy to walk around and difficult to get lost. Winding its way through the middle is the Arno River with a series of bridges crossing it including the famous Ponte Vecchio.

Quaint little jewellery shops are crowded on top of the bridge, hanging over its edge precariously. As I stand on the Ponte Vecchio I try to imagine it without tourists, to get a sense of what life might have been like during the Medici period.

Everywhere I go there are police so I feel completely safe. Florentine people are really friendly and incredibly proud of their city and its glorious history. So far, I have only dealt with lovely people who are completely comfortable with foreigners—novel for Italy. The weather is much milder than in Abruzzo, which is a welcome change.

The walk to my language school is about fifteen to twenty minutes. I can go the direct way, cutting through narrow city streets, but most days I choose the scenic route. I pass all the major tourist sites along the way—San Lorenzo church; the beautiful *duomo* with its amazing coloured marble in a geometric delight of pink, green and white that looks like a giant wedding cake; and the Piazza Della Signorina.

My school is directly opposite Santa Croce church, on two floors of an old *palazzo*. I am in a small class of five with Mario who is Swiss, Martin from Ireland, Nicole, a Swedish university student, and Takako, a Japanese woman. We all get along well and crave our coffee at morning break. We are at the same language level but are here for different reasons. As I am an English language teacher, I'm really enjoying being on the other side, watching how other language teachers plan and deliver their lessons and most importantly feeling and experiencing what my students do. I am constantly reflecting on my own teaching and how students must feel when they are in my class.

I learnt Italian at secondary school. I use the term learnt liberally, as I misbehaved so badly in class the teacher sent a letter home to my parents. My father, who never raised his voice at us, told me that of his five sons, not one had a letter like that sent home from school. He never expected it to come from his only daughter. Looking back, I was trying to hide my 'Italianness' by being a cocky brat in class, too cool to learn Italian. I remember my Italian teacher berating me in front of the class for not pronouncing my surname correctly. 'You should be proud of where you come from, Angela,' said Mrs Di Stefano.

The way we say our surname in Australia is not the way our relatives in Italy say it. Years ago we changed the pronunciation to make it sound more Australian and easier for other people to pronounce. My brother Peter, when he left Geelong, started referring to himself with the correct pronunciation. At work I like to use the correct pronunciation, but Geelong is a small town and when you are the only family with the name Di Sciascio, it's a bit hard to change your identity. I recall being at university in Melbourne and phoning Felicetta and Joe, our good friends from Abruzzo, who lived near the university residence. I left a message on their phone saying I would be coming for dinner.

They told me they played the message over and over, laughing at how I pronounced *DiSasio* instead of *Di Shiashio*. I was embarrassed and ashamed, while they were so proud. Now that I am here, I love the sound of my name. It is poetic and a marker of where in Italy I come from.

In my free time, I sit in a piazza for hours observing the goings on. I see a new mum dressed for the catwalk pushing a designer pram with a designer baby asleep in it. This is the land of metallic sneakers, often with high wedge heels, matching accessories and loads of jewellery. Patent leather has a huge market here—anything that glimmers and shines. All over town I see people casually riding bicycles. Most of the historical centre is free of cars, which encourages cycling and makes walking around a pleasure. The bikes have wide spongy seats and baskets on the front; they're mechanically uncomplicated and elegant. Florentines glide rather than ride.

Going to school every day again makes me reflect on my own schooling and that of my father. I have been blessed with a thorough education, complete with university undergraduate and postgraduate studies. My father on the other hand only had a few years of schooling. When World War II started all the teachers, nurses and other such professionals were recruited to serve their country. This meant that Capoposta had no school for many years. Not long after the war members of the community lobbied the authorities to rectify this. After proving that Capoposta could guarantee twenty students, a room for the school and lodging for the teacher, the municipality paid for a teacher. A young lady from Guardiagrele was sent to Capoposta to educate the young, and the old. She spent several years living in my great uncle's home amongst a grateful people. My father's cousin Biasetto recently saw the aged teacher and spoke with tears in his eyes as he related to me their conversation together.

Festa della Donna

ALL OVER THE city there are stallholders selling
sprigs of mimosa flowers. Men will give these
sprigs to women to honour International Women's
day, *Festa della Donna*. Throughout the city museums
have opened their doors to women for free. I plan to
take full advantage of the opportunity and will visit
the most feminine exhibits—porcelain, costumes and
gardens—in keeping with the spirit of the day.

But first I am going on an excursion with my fellow
students and one of the teachers to the *Cappelle Medici*.
The *Cappelle Medici* was the private mausoleum of
the Medici family and includes a spectacular use of
dark, sombre marble mosaics encircling the walls
and sarcophagi below a wonderfully painted dome.
The mosaics on the altar are so fine, the integration

of colours so delicate, it is like looking at a painting. Next to the old chapel is the *Cappelle Nuova*, which has an unfinished Michelangelo design. But it is the sculptures that capture my imagination. My guide book mentions something about the grotesque female figurines and suggests perhaps Michelangelo never saw a naked woman. I giggle upon entering the chapel, immediately seeing what the writer meant as I observe the strangely located breasts and well developed six-packs of the sculptures within.

Afterwards, my classmate Takaka and I go to San Lorenzo market, Florence's huge indoor fresh produce market and an absolute dream to wander through. Florentines love their tripe so there are tripe stalls everywhere. Lining the aisles are butcher stalls with soft pink meat and dark-red giant T-bone steaks ready for the famous *bistecca alla fiorentina*, a steak weighing up to two kilograms.

The produce is different here from that in Abruzzo. In Abruzzo now there would be mountains of *verdure*, leafy green vegetables. Here I find only one stall with broccollini, but plenty of asparagus, cabbage (the famous *cavolo nero*) and artichokes. There are fish stalls, dried fruit stalls, nut stalls, porcini mushroom stalls, cheese stalls, prosciutto and salami stalls, citrus stalls, vegetable stalls, fresh fruit stalls and sweets stalls. All around me people are buying their goods and I spot a group of nuns in habits buying meat for the weekend.

I say goodbye to Takaka and head off in search of lunch. I have read about a fantastic *trattoria* near the market that opens only for lunch and serves locals and market workers. I decide to hunt it out.

Tucked in a narrow street next to the market lies the discreetly marked Trattoria Mario. There are already people queued outside. I go in to put my name down and as I'm on my own I get seated straightaway. I take a deep breath and examine my surroundings, a narrow restaurant with an open kitchen and a bar down one side. It is packed with eager customers huddled together over tiny tables, just big enough for everyone's plates and carafes of wine. Customers sit on little three-legged stools and winter jackets line the walls. The place is humming with the beat of good food, fast service, contented customers and a charismatic owner who manages the waiting crowds outside with consummate diplomacy. Italians don't like to wait, but for good food they make an exception.

I sit down at a table with three locals and say hello. In half English, half Italian, we share what we have done for the day and then let each other eat in peace. The lady next to me is ploughing her way through one of those huge Florentine T-bone steaks. The waiter arrives and tells me the day's pasta menu. He speaks so fast I don't catch much but I recognise *tortolloni con pomodoro* so order that. To wash it down I selected a quarter-litre *vino rosso*. Within a minute it seems my piping hot plate of fresh *tortolloni* (*oni* = large, *ini* = small, so picture giant *tortellini*) with a light tomato sauce arrives. The pasta is fresh and silky but with the right amount of bite. The filling has a perfect balance of spinach and cheese. When I finish Fillippo the waiter returns and rapidly lists the main courses for the day. Again I don't get much except *trippo* and *vitello*. Definitely not wanting tripe, I opt for the veal. Thin slices of juicy roasted meat with braised greens arrive and I leave the restaurant content and knowing I will return, like many of that day's customers, for another meal at Mario's.

Feeling sated, a pair of shoes in a window catches my eye and I wander into a leather shop. After some clever salesmanship I leave not with the pair I spotted but with another, a pair of beautifully soft black leather boots. Thoughts of how I might fit them into my already overloaded luggage quickly fade—there really is nothing like Italian leather footwear.

In keeping with Lady's Day I then go to one of the major museums to take advantage of the free tickets. I head over the Arno to *Pallazzo Pitti* to see the Borboli Gardens, the Costume Museum and Porcelain Museum. Girly things on a girly day. The costume museum has painstakingly hand-crafted ladies' and men's clothes spanning the last few hundred years. The detail, hand stitching, embroidery and lace work are so delicate but I can't help thinking what a pity it is people couldn't put the same design and detail into the hygiene and sewerage systems in that time.

The garments are tiny. I am reminded of the delicate dress we have at home that once belonged to my great grandmother in the nineteenth century. As children we were fascinated by such a petite garment and wondered at who might have worn it.

I walk out of the museum into the grand sixteenth-century Borboli Gardens, a sea of fountains, ponds, grassed areas, tiered pathways and dramatic views of the Florentine skyline. There is peace here. No traffic, just the sound of birds and the splash of water in fountains. I bask in the serenity then begin walking higher in the gardens towards the Porcelain Museum. The climb to the top affords spectacular views of the 'backyard' of Florence. Behind the *Pitti* lies a large olive grove and country houses that rest on the edge of the city. Before me is the type of view you see on the cover of books about Tuscany, a villa with a worn yellow/orange render, dark-green cypress pine trees reaching for the sky, and rolling hills. Cliched yet perfect.

The Porcelain Museum and its exquisite collection of fine china remind me of the beautiful Italian coffee set my parents received for their wedding over fifty years ago. It's white with an intricate gold design and holds pride of place in Mum's cabinet, to be brought out only on special occasions. My brother Peter and I often joke about who wants to inherit it more, he or I. He usually wins, although I know my niece Koko has her eye on it too. How they would adore the fine beauty expressed here on the dinner sets of the Medicis.

As I wander home through the now familiar streets of San Giovanni and San Lorenzo I stop at my local bar for a well-deserved glass of *prosecco*. While I wasn't given a sprig of mimosa, I did get to experience a day filled with beauty that I will remember for a long time.

It is tiring constantly thinking in another language. My brain is continually on overload and I find myself becoming frustrated when I can't express myself in public with words we've just covered in vocabulary class. Despite this I have a sneaking suspicion it is actually working and every day I feel a little more confident. Being the child of a migrant makes for a confusing sense of identity; some days I feel Italian, others I feel Australian. Mostly I feel like a perplexing mix of the two. I'm not sure if it is the classes but I am starting to feel more connected to Italy.

Dad embraced the Australian way of life and let Mum decide when it came to how my brothers and I were raised. We always knew we were half Italian. Family photos would arrive sent from Italy and we received letters a couple of times a year. We had wonderful family friends who were Italian, other migrants from Dad's village or nearby, but we never spoke Italian as children, we didn't hang out at the Italian club, we didn't go to Saturday Italian school like other Italian kids, we didn't make salami or wine, have lavish first communions or follow feast days.

When I was growing up it was decidedly uncool to be a 'wog'. My brothers and I were picked on at school because of our funny surname and I remember a day when one of my brothers refused to eat the pasta served for dinner. 'I don't want to eat this wog food!' he snapped. Mum was furious but Dad calmly replied, 'That's fine,' and asked Mum to get my brother something else. Today when he recounts this story my brother has tears in his eyes from the shame. I share his shame for the culture and traditions we have squandered. Now I must play catch-up.

Florentine steaks

1 T-bone steak per 2 people
radicchio, chopped
rocket
salt and cracked pepper
olive oil
parmesan

Use large and thick good-quality T-Bone steaks.
Cook without seasoning over coals or on a grill until done to your liking. Serve on a wooden chopping board, cutting and serving the meat at the table.
A big Florentine steak can feed at least two people.

I had this steak with chopped radicchio and rocket.
I added some radicchio and rocket to my plate and

then the sliced steak was served on top. I seasoned the meat with salt and cracked pepper, drizzled the plate with good-quality olive oil and topped the dish with shaved parmesan cheese. The bitterness of the radicchio, the peppery rocket and the sharp cheese went so perfectly with the steak.

This is a fantastic dinner party meal as guests can construct their dish at the table.

Food, soccer
and *stranieri*

MOST MORNINGS I wake to the bells of San
Lorenzo church just one block from my apartment. On this morning, however, I wake at 4.30 am to
the beep beep of SMS messages. As I drag myself from
my slumber I remember, it is my birthday.

I buy a packet of Baci chocolates to share with
the class at school and when I arrive two birthday
cards from the family are there to greet me. I decide to
celebrate with three friends from my school—Nicole,
Pascal and Janet. As they are all young university
students forced to count every penny, I follow Italian
practice and invite them to dinner as my guests.

We meet in the middle of the Ponte Vecchio and
walk together to a family *trattoria* in Oltrano. As we

sit scanning the menu we suddenly realise we have all forgotten our dictionaries. The options before us are extremely complicated, littered with words none of us recognise. Rather than be defeated we decide to all choose a dish we don't know and be surprised. I secretly hope whatever mine is, it does not involve offal.

Our waiter is a dotty old man who keeps forgetting our order, coming back to check it several times. Then again, perhaps his memory isn't as bad as it seems; each time he takes the opportunity to put his arms around Janet, a gorgeous 20-something Hungarian. While trying to ignore him we notice the man at the table next to us. Before him is a plate piled high with fresh broad beans, still in their long pods. As we watch he proceeds to sprinkle salt on his plate, shell the beans and dip each in the salt before popping them into his mouth with pieces of *pecorino* cheese. Our meals don't prove quite as entertaining but they are a success. Dessert is the highlight, however: lemon sorbet served in a hollowed out lemon straight from the freezer. Delicious.

By the end of the meal we are all a bit tipsy on rum baba, wine and the delicious stickiness of *limoncello* liqueur. The waiter is a little more than tipsy too. He sits down heavily at our table and proceeds to write up our bill without any apparent reference to what we have eaten. Thankfully his drunken mathematics works to my advantage. We wander back over the Ponte Vecchio, now quiet and eerily absent of tourists, through the Piazza Republica and past the illuminated carousel back to our houses and our waiting beds.

My Florence home is close to the train station and there is an obvious presence of new migrants in my neighbourhood. It doesn't matter where you are in the world; migrants are always found near the train stations. In side streets near my apartment are dark internet cafes acting as call centres and hang-outs for the many men, always men; there are few women. There are several little take-away shops in the area too, selling an eclectic mix of food. In Australia, the Greeks learned to sell dim sims and fish and chips alongside their souvlaki. Here Italian pizza sits beside curry and kebabs. I recently read in the local English-language paper that in Lucca the council has banned the opening of any new kebab shops within its ancient walls.

I recall a conversation I overheard recently as I sat in the beautiful Piazza Michelangelo. Set in the hills above Otrarno, it has a picture-perfect view over the Arno, its bridges and the city. As I admired the view I overheard a conversation next to me. A man was telling his friend how different the city was fifteen years ago, '… there were Italians everywhere, especially in the market stalls'.

'There were Italians everywhere …' I think about that statement now. Globalisation has changed the face of world and with it the face of Italy is changing. I know that Italians in general are very frightened of the waves of *stranieri* entering their country and are saddened by the changes happening around them. They are very untrusting of these people and often crime sprees or problems are blamed on the Albanians, Romanians or Africans. For me, used to not only living in a melting pot but indeed being a product of it, I find their fears unwarranted. Perhaps the sentiment was the same in Australia in the 1950s. Did my dad change his name to fit in? How did Valentino become Wally?

It's hard to imagine the poverty and desperation of the millions of people left behind by the devastation of World War II. When the war ended my father's family had not one cent between them. No cash. Nothing. There was no water (women carried large copper pots on their heads to and from the communal fountain), no electricity, no machines to help with the harvest, no cars, no road (only a track), no privacy (multiple families shared one house) and no jobs. Only their land, their animals, their house and their sheer determination to survive got them through. Other families were not so fortunate, still labouring under a feudal system or living as artisans in nearby towns with no garden, pig, chickens and cows to feed their families.

By 1951 my dad had had enough and seeing no future, no opportunities and no joy in the land of his birth he joined the hordes of young men who ventured across the seas to America, Argentina or Australia.

It took some time after deciding to actually leave for my dad to get the courage to tell his parents. Then there were the months of planning. He had to save enough money for the journey, then go through the application processes and mentally prepare to cross the world to a completely unknown land. Dad's family was upset that he was leaving them and his mother cried constantly. They would miss him, his music and importantly, the contribution his labour made to their survival. His father understood; he himself had lived and worked in America for fifteen years before World War I. However, Nonno Mattia always expected my dad to return home. So did Dad.

Dad had his medical checks and an interview with an Australian immigration official who wrote on his application document, 'Willing to accept any kind of unskilled work anywhere. He appears to be an average type of rural worker.' He then stamped it, 'recommended'.

Leaving behind his beloved *Bianchoni* accordion, Dad packed his belongings into a brown suitcase, wrote his name on it with whitewash and, with his best friend Silvino, left his home, his family, his village and his country. He would never see his parents again and would not return to his village for another twenty-two years. The evening before his departure, there was a *festa* at my Nonno's. The house was filled with relatives and friends who came to wish Valentino farewell. My uncle cries when he recalls this *festa*. Saying goodbye must have been horrendous. It is difficult to imagine what emotions my dad was feeling as he embarked on his journey.

Dad and Silvino did, however, have an adventurous few days before they journeyed from Naples. They spent a night in Chieti and went to the cinema, which would have been a magical experience for them. From there they caught the train to Pescara and then continued on to Naples where they boarded the *Florentia*, an ex-Panamanian military transport ship. Two hundred and eighty men were crammed into lower deck cabins with no air-conditioning or ventilation. For someone who had never left their province a journey across the seas, through the Suez Canal and down to Australia must have been both exciting and arduous. The journey was long, at times boring, and the mostly single men spent their time talking and getting up to mischief.

My dad and his friends had run out of money by the time they reached Fremantle. Perhaps the large Italian population in Fremantle is in part due to the fact that some just couldn't last the distance to Melbourne, while others were keen to make money in the first place they could. In the autumn of 1952, after forty-two days at sea, the *Florentia* arrived at Victoria Dock, Melbourne. For some Australia would become their permanent home. Others would find the distance from family too hard to bear, and after a few years many returned to Italy.

After disembarking, hundreds of eager migrants were bussed to the train station, where they were given a bread roll before boarding a train to Bonegilla Migrant Camp in northern Victoria. As the Red Rattler rocked its way north Dad and his friends got their first glimpses of their new land through the open windows of the carriage. They were amazed at how many people waved to them, and upon hearing crows for the first time thought they were the bleats of sheep. They arrived tired but excited at the camp early on the morning of Anzac Day. Later they joined in a rabbit drive and had a lot of fun catching rabbits by hand, a skill I imagine must have been quite welcome in Australia at the time.

There was little to do that first month. The camp had an employment office and every day men were matched to jobs around Victoria. Dad was eager to be allocated to one but in the meantime he and his friends passed the time learning English, playing music, or hunting for rabbits on neighbouring farms. In late May Dad moved to Somers Camp on the Mornington Peninsula. For him, it was much better than Bonegilla; there was more to do and it was more family oriented. Dad was now desperate to get work outside of the camp and on 26 June, approximately two months after arriving in Australia, he did his first day of paid work in Australia, earning one pound sterling for cutting timber on a pig farm.

Dad turned his hand to almost anything, doing a stint at the Ford car factory in Geelong, building timber frames for houses, working on a country road repair gang, and driving trucks. One of the most memorable jobs was the eighteen months spent working twelve-hour shifts building Avalon Airport. During the construction hundreds of migrant men camped on the Avalon plain for months on end. Dad recalls these days with fondness, perhaps because the camp cook was from Abruzzo, trained at Villa Santa Maria cooking school.

It was at one of these early jobs that Dad was christened Wally, after the popular *Herald* cartoon at the time, *Wally and the Major*. A foreman decided that Valentino was not the name for Dad, so dubbed him Wally. Whether this was motivated by ease of pronunciation, prejudice, ignorance or arrogance we'll never know. But somehow my father's desire to be called Tino was overturned. Wally stuck. It still sticks.

In Capoposta, they are not so worried by the Albanians as the waves of English buying up the old farmhouses. In Ascigno, the village next to Capoposta, there are four or five houses now owned by *Inglese*. Their arrival has led to much speculation. It seems the English prefer to buy houses that are a little isolated rather than ones close to other dwellings. My cousin asks me, 'Why don't they want to live near other people? Italians don't like to be away from other people, they prefer houses near people.' Perhaps therein lies the difference. I see these English at the Casoli market. They stand out with their casual dress, white skins, and taste for beer in the middle of the day. I wonder how long it will be before they assimilate and whether it bothers them that they don't yet fit in.

One Sunday I find myself at the main train station. I had planned to return to Capoposta for Easter but as I stand at the computerised self-service ticket machine my selections are all coming up negative. I have left my run too late. The hordes of southern Italians working in the north have beaten me to the last seats and now I'm panicking because I can't work out what to do. The thought of spending Easter alone in Florence doesn't appeal.

I make a few phone calls and discover that my cousin Anna, a school teacher in Bergamo, near Milan, is not returning to Abruzzo for Easter either. As soon as I confirm that there are seats available I buy my ticket to Bergamo. I'm still sorting things at the ticket office when I hear an almighty commotion and see people running. A quick look at one of the platforms reveals riot police and a large group of people, mostly men, attacking each other. I'm alarmed and then I remember—Genova is playing Florence in the soccer.

By the time I'm finished the commotion is over and the train station has returned to its usual mix of lost and amazed tourists, rushing commuters, beggars and pickpockets.

Easter with Anna is celebrated at her best friend Giovanna's house. Giovanna is from Palermo and her parents are visiting so I get to experience a traditional Sicilian menu in a northern city. We start with an *antipasto* selection of crostini, dried bread, olives and tuna, fried eggplant, sundried tomatoes and salami, along with a fennel, pear and cashew salad made by my cousin. For the *primo*, we eat *annelleti*, pasta shaped like little rings, with a rich tomato sauce and peas baked in the oven. The *secondo* is roast rabbit and lamb served with potatoes. We follow this with homemade gelato and fresh fruit, finishing with cake and *spumante*—a long but delicious meal in delightful company.

Pasticci
Abruzzese Easter pastries, sometimes known as fiadoni

Filling
   1 kg fresh *pecorino*, grated
   5 eggs
   2 tbspn grated *grana padana* cheese

Mix ingredients together with a spoon.

Pastry

3 eggs (add more if needed for the amount of flour)

150 ml oil

150 ml water

150 ml milk

3 cups plain flour

3 cups self-raising flour

pinch of salt

Mix the wet ingredients together. Put the flours on a pasta board, add a pinch of salt and make a well. Add the wet ingredients to the well and then use a fork to gradually incorporate the flour to make a soft dough. Knead gently. Halve the dough and then use a rolling pin to roll out to large pizza size, dusting with flour as you go. Cut into pieces and, using a pasta machine, roll out pastry until quite thin. Cut pastry into 10-cm squares. Place a spoonful of filling mixture in the centre of each pastry round and fold the corners towards the centre to make a little parcel. Place the folded side down on a tray lined with baking paper. Brush with milk and snip the top of the pastry with a pair of scissors. Bake in a 180°C oven for about 15 minutes, until brown. The cheese should pop through the hole like a volcano.

You can also make a sweet version, where sugar is added to the cheese mixture, but I much prefer the savoury ones.

I have loved my time in Florence but after a month away I am ready to return to Abruzzo. I make sure I have crossed off all the major things I wanted to see and experience in Florence and promise myself I will return. A few of us are finishing our courses on the same day so we decide to go out as a farewell. It is a little strange saying goodbye to people from all over the world knowing that we will probably never see each other again. As to my Italian, I am very happy with what I've learnt and while I may not be fluent I do feel I now have a good foundation for the remainder of my year. Before leaving I purchase a couple of good grammar books and set myself a little program of self-study. It will be interesting to see whether I stick with it.

Before going back to Abruzzo I spend three days in Lucca, an ancient walled city about an hour from Florence by train. It is a compact city and very few cars are allowed within the walled area. Most people get around on foot or by bicycle. The first thing I notice is the serenity. There is no hustle or bustle. Everyone moves at such a peaceful pace. I literally see people smelling the roses. It is an interesting contrast to the flurry of Florence, not to mention life back home. People never *passeggiare* in Australia; there they always walk with a purpose—to exercise, to work, to get the baby asleep, to buy milk—never just for walking's sake.

I spend three whole days wandering through this gorgeous town with its circular streets, odd-shaped piazzas and elegant locals. There is a wide path on top of the ancient wall and one Sunday morning I spend a lovely couple of hours walking the rim of the city, peering over the edge at the goings on below. There are so many people out enjoying the spring weather, indulging in a peaceful stroll before Sunday lunch with family.

Lucca is the birthplace of Puccini and my hotel room looks over a tiny piazza next to Puccini's house; a bronze statue of the man sitting casually in a chair, cigarette dangling from between his fingers, stands in the middle of the piazza. In every photo or picture I see of Puccini there is a cigarette either in his hand or in his mouth. Not surprisingly, throat cancer got him in the end.

Lucca has a permanent Puccini music festival. Every night of the year a concert is held in honour of Puccini in the *Chiesa Di San Giovanni e Reparata*. I go to concert number 899—a Puccini 'n' Jazz night. Sitting in this historic church, listening to modern jazz interpretations of some of Puccini's glorious music, I revel in the moment and in how lucky I am to be here.

There is an old saying in Lucca: '*Chi va a Lucca e non mangia il buccellato è come se non ci fosse stato*' or, in English: 'Going to Lucca and not eating the *buccellato* is like never being there.' *Buccellato* is a yeast fruit cake flavoured with anise seeds. It is just perfect with coffee, a delightful mix of spice and fruit in sweet bread-like dough. I even sample *buccellato* stuffed with *semifreddo* and have to close my eyes to soak up the joy.

During my stay I try some pasta dishes particular to the area. Delicious *lasagnette*, a pasta shape of eight- to ten-centimetre strips about two- to three centimetres wide, served with asparagus and butter sauce, and the most delightful ricotta tortellini with a butter and zucchini sauce. Other typical Tuscan dishes on offer include *ribolitta* (like minestrone but thick with beans and bread), *pappa al pomodoro* (bread and tomato soup), pasta with *ragu* of *cinghiale* (wild boar), and *crostini* with *fegato* (dried bread with liver).

Unfortunately, eating out here is quite expensive, although I can't walk past a restaurant without reading the menu. One evening I treat myself to dinner at the famous *Buca di Sant'Antonio* restaurant, which has been operating since 1782. I have a mouth watering roast baby goat from the Garfagnana mountains. It is so tasty I forgo good table manners to lick my fingers in delight.

It sounds ludicrous but I often plan my food days in advance, desperate to try the many diverse dishes on offer. I simply cannot move through this great land and not experience all the wondrous variety, even if some of it isn't to my liking. Some might even cost me a king's ransom. These are sacrifices I am very willing to make.

Blooms, bounty and bliss of spring

I RETURN FROM TUSCANY late at night. As I drive home to Capoposta from the train station in Pescara I can see by my headlights that the trees have changed. I wake the next day to spring and breathe in the changes all around me. The sky is a clear, crisp blue and the air refreshing and clean. As I look over the valley I see fields of hay and grain bursting with life after the March rains. In the olive groves delicate white wild flowers grow in the shade of olive branches. Most have been pruned by now but there is still work to be done on the trees. There are wildflowers everywhere. On my walk I collect a posy of at least ten different blossoms, a rainbow of spring colours—yellow, pink, violet, orange and white. As I type the posy is in a vase on my desk reminding me where I am. The birds are chirpier than usual too, and my aunt's kitchen garden is bursting with colour and life.

Favetta

This is made with fresh young broad beans straight from the vegie patch.

> onion, finely chopped
> fennel, finely chopped
> rosemary, chopped
> olive oil
> chicory, finely chopped
> pinch of salt
> 2 cups broad beans (podded, blanched and
>   skin removed)
> *pecorino romano* cheese, grated

Sauté onion, fennel and rosemary in olive oil until soft. Add chicory and stir until the chicory has softened. Add a pinch of salt. Cook on low for about 5 minutes. Add broad beans and continue to cook on low until soft. Serve with grated *pecorino romano* cheese as a first course instead of pasta.

The balance of ingredients is important here. It is a delicate mix of gentle aniseed from the fennel, aromatic rosemary, the sweetness of the beans and the bitterness of the chicory.

Being home again, I am keen to reinstate my daily walks. As I climb the rise to Ascigno I come to a little intersection and pass a sight not uncommon here. On the wall of one of the houses is a small shrine to the Virgin Mary, the Madonna. The shrine is simple but clearly well tended, with a small fresco, candles and flowers. The first time I saw one of these shrines was in Rome; I was so taken aback I took photos. I've now seen possibly hundreds and in the strangest of places, all carefully cared for by the people living nearby. The one in Ascigno is particularly beautiful and I pause to admire it each time I pass.

Italians have a deep sense of religion. They take their saints, sacraments and the Pope very seriously, and the Madonna is truly idolised. In Australia, with its Irish influences, Catholicism tends to be a more insular affair confined to the church. By contrast, Italians proudly display their religion in the streets yet rarely attend Mass.

At the intersection you can go straight and walk through the village, or veer right to pass the house where Nonna Chiara was born. In the middle of the intersection is a big tree with sweeping branches that reminds me of peppercorns back home. Under it today sits an old man in a rickety old chair. He is dressed in his flat Abruzzese cap, wearing an old blue coat similar to the ones worn by many farmers here and by boilermakers back in Australia. Beside him is a ten-foot pile of olive prunings. He is slowly working his way through them, carefully cleaning the leaves from the branches to make kindling. I look at him sitting peacefully in the shade of this old tree with the Madonna watching over him as he works and wonder how many days it will take him to get through the pile. He waves hello as I pass by. I want so much to take a photo but can't bring myself to intrude on his peace.

I have the spring sun on my back as I walk, taking in the view across to Casoli. I am warm and cosy and thankfully for once haven't encountered any angry dogs. About six weeks ago I met an old friend of my father's and promised to visit again. However, soon after I came down with the flu, then it was raining and cold, and then I went to Florence. Today I must keep the promise I made to this old man and his wife so long ago.

When I approach their house, they are both gently toiling in their beautiful vegetable garden. They are well into their eighties yet their garden still sustains them. They greet me as old friends and we go inside for coffee.

Giuseppe speaks a little English. I ask where he learnt and he tells me he was a prisoner of war for several years, spending time in South Africa and two years in England in a POW camp. Remarkably, at eight-six years of age he still remembers enough of what he learned all those years ago that we can talk together. My month in Florence has also helped; I can understand much more of what people say to me now, even in dialect. I still sound like a bumbling fool but we are laughing and happy. Giuseppe comments that at least animals all over the world have the same language. I remark that this may be so, then explain that language descriptions for the same sound sometimes differ. For instance, in English we say *cockadoodledoo* for the rooster's morning call, whereas in Italian it is *yicketyyicketyyeee*. He looks at me very strangely and scratches his head until I realise he thinks I'm saying that in Australia the chickens actually do speak a different language. I finally work out a way to describe what I mean and we laugh even harder. After coffee and the obligatory slices of delicious Abruzzese Easter biscotti I leave the comfort of their welcome, promising to return.

After a month in Tuscany, I am back in the land of spaghetti *chitarra* with a tomato sauce, strictly no buttery ones. Zio Alberto groans any time my aunt dares to make pasta without tomatoes. I have even seen him make the sign of the cross when a dish of *macheroni chitarra con sugo* is placed on the table in front of him. His behaviour reminds me of Dad. If it isn't tomato based then it isn't a real sauce, according to any good Abruzzese. Should we dare venture outside these boundaries back in Australia, we have to make two dishes—one *rosso* (red, with tomato) for the traditionalists (mainly Dad) and one *bianco* (white, meaning pasta without tomato). The same rule applies here, so to compensate my aunt makes sure she never goes two days without *pasta pomodoro*. Perhaps it's my father's influence, but I must confess I was desperate for *pasta pomodoro alla Abruzzese* by my last week in Florence.

As I finish writing this I can hear my uncle playing his piano accordion downstairs. Perhaps all my stories of Dad's playing have inspired him.

Sugo pomodoro
Basic tomato pasta sauce

> oil
> 2 or more whole garlic cloves, smashed lightly
> 1 small onion
> carrot and celery (optional)
> 1 bottle tomato sauce (see note on page 98)
> 1 bunch fresh mixed herbs

You need to start this sauce well before cooking the pasta, as it will take far longer than the pasta. Add a generous slurp of oil to a pan and gently saute whole garlic cloves (at least 2), one whole small onion, or half if larger, and a couple of pieces of carrot and celery for flavour if you wish. Add tomato sauce (see note overleaf) and a bunch of fresh mixed herbs tied with string. Simmer covered for about 30 minutes for maximum flavour, less if you don't have time. The sauce is ready when the oil splits. There should be generous amount of oil sitting on top of the sauce. If it's too dry, add a little pasta water. Season at the end before adding to the pasta.

A note on tomatoes for pasta

Use bottled tomatoes that have been preserved as they have been minced, possibly with basil. Bertolli Provisto Sugo Classico or De Cecco Rustica are the best bottled sauce brands I have found in Australia. They are most like the preserved tomatoes my mother makes. Avoid any bottled sauce that looks smooth like tomato sauce, and don't buy bottled tomatoes that have extras added or are flavoured. For quick pasta sauces I always use canned whole tomatoes. For a basic sauce for four people, you will need two 400 g cans. The best way to prepare canned tomatoes is to open them into a large bowl and, using your hands, crush them so they end up a fine pulpy mass.

Sometimes you may need to add some sugar to a tomato sauce. This depends on the acid level of the tomatoes. If it is too tangy on your tongue, add a pinch or two of sugar.

Le Marche and Umbria—Roman trails

THE SKY IS BLUE over the Adriatic as I sit on a rocky shore, squinting in the sunlight and watching the water glisten. I am in Fano, a smallish city of about 60,000 people on the coast between Ancona and Rimini in the region of Le Marche and it is beautiful. My cousin Giacinto's home is my home now for the next few weeks before I head further north.

Fano is a very old Roman township with a beautifully preserved historical centre surrounded by a Roman wall perched on the edge of a gorgeous beach, and all just a twenty-minute walk from Giacinto's house.

Saturday is market day. We get up early and head into the town square where the main market is held every Saturday and Wednesday. Italian markets are like large department stores. You can buy everything from buckets to pasta machines, underwear, designer clothes, olives from Puglia, citrus from Sicily, and fresh fish caught that morning. Like most Italians Giacinto buys his everyday items at the local street markets and it is a joy watching him astutely select fruit, vegetables and fish from his favourite sellers.

My cousin's wife Madalena is an expert cook and my cousin Giacinto an expert eater. Madalena is enjoying having such an eager student in her kitchen and we have great fun cooking together. She makes fresh pasta at least once a week. Her pasta board is hidden in a wonderfully handy spot just under the kitchen table so she can whip it out and have a batch of pasta kneaded in what seems like the blink of an eye.

Cooking with Madalena has taught me the importance of good-quality flour, especially when making pasta without eggs, and that even though it sounds so daunting, making fresh pasta can be quite effortless. To do so, you need the best quality hard wheat flour you can get. Madalena has a special bag used only for pasta. This bag of precious dust, her well-worn pasta board, rolling pin, pasta rolling machine and thirty-year-old *chitarra* are her most important cooking tools.

Together we make *cavatelli*, a variety of pasta from Puglia made with just water and flour. Traditionally eggs were only used for special occasions and are more prominent in pasta from the north. The *cavatelli* shape is very simple to form and looks a little like a cross between *orecchiete* and an open penne. We serve it with fresh *carciofi*, artichoke. I've not really enjoyed artichoke up until now but I've learnt a secret: you simply must put some mint with it when you sauté—it is a wonderful marriage of flavours.

While in Fano I am introduced to *piadina* bread, which is bit like a tortilla or roti and is found in Le Marche and Emilia Romagna along with a few other places in Italy. It is particularly delicious served hot with *scarmorza* cheese and sautéed silverbeet. While out walking I buy a freshly made *piadina* served with slices of roasted *porchetta*, all salty and juicy with hints of fennel, garlic, pepper, caramelised skin and tender pork meat. I am quite simply unable to resist buying a *porchetta* sandwich at any market I go to. This is decadent in the extreme but the *porchetta* here is unlike any we have in Australia.

Timballo as made by Madalena
Abruzzese lasagna

> fresh pasta dough (see recipe, page 38)
> *sugo agnello* (see recipe, page 18)
> 200 g beef mince
> parmesan, grated
> mozzarella, grated

Make fresh pasta dough and rest it for 30 minutes. Use a machine to make the pasta strips. Pass the pasta through the machine. Use setting number 1 three times, then number 3 once, then 4 once, then 5 once, then 6 once.

For a *timballo* you will need a good *sugo agnello*, or lamb *sugo*, but take the lamb out of the sauce at the end of the cooking process.

Form tiny meatballs using the beef mince, and fry separately.

With a bowl of grated parmesan cheese and another bowl of grated mozzarella cheese at the ready, place a few sheets of the pasta into boiling water that has been salted and oiled. When the water returns to the boil, remove the sheets and place in a bowl with cold water and then lay a cloth over the top.

Start preparing the *timballo*. Add some *sugo* to the bottom of a lasagne tray, then place the first layer of pasta over the sauce. Add some of the meatballs, parmesan and mozzarella. Then keep repeating until pasta is finished and the tray is full. Never put pasta layers on top of each other without any sauce. Cook the pasta in the boiling water as you go, otherwise it will be too hard to handle. This dish is best made with two people!

Bake for 30 minutes at 200°C.

It can be prepared ahead and frozen, then taken out to bake when you need it.

Giacinto and I talk for hours about Dad, Australia and our family. A couple of years ago, in celebration of his retirement, Giacinto visited Australia. We compare our cultures and our experiences. Giacinto recalls a conversation with my father over twenty years ago. Despite outside perceptions Italians have quite small families— most of my relatives have no more than three children, and even three is rare. My father is therefore seen as a curiosity for having had six. Giacinto remembers asking Dad why he had so many offspring. My father replied that he never wanted to feel the loneliness he experienced when he migrated to Australia. A large close family ensured he would never be alone again. I suspect my mother's adherence to Catholic doctrine also played a part.

There is nothing my father likes more than to be surrounded by family. He worked side by side with two of his sons in the family business and today my parents, myself and three of my brothers all live within one hundred metres of each other. I am glad Dad's dream to never be alone has come true.

I am captivated by the Roman doors in this remarkable city. The main gate into Fano is a giant arch of marble. Just inside the entrance is a little hole tucked inside the wall of the arch. It is here that in ancient times women would put their unwanted babies, who would then be collected by nuns to care for. Underneath is another little nook where people put donations of money for the care of these babies.

Winding my way down through the town I end up at the beach. Everything shuts down over winter but as I walk past, many of the cafes and bars are polishing up in readiness for the season. Italian beaches are nothing like those I'm used to in Australia. There are private beaches called a *bagno* or *lido* where you have to rent an umbrella and booth. There are bars, games areas and walking paths to the shore so you don't ever have to touch the sand or rocks.

One bright day I set off for Urbino, another walled town, this time on top of a hill. The bus trip alone is incredible, passing through the Le Marche countryside with is rolling hills, sprawling green fields and tall cypress trees. The fields here are larger than in Abruzzo and so the countryside has a less patchwork, cluttered look. I can't get over the vivid greens of spring.

Once in Urbino I visit the *Pallazo Ducale* hoping to see one of its treasures, Raphael's *Portrait of a Gentlewoman*. The hands of this fine lady are so exquisite, so lifelike, that it is like looking at a photo. I lean closer to admire them, becoming so absorbed that I forget myself and set off the alarms! Embarrassed, I scuttle away to another room before I can be found out.

After admiring the wonders of Raphael, and almost getting arrested, I take a wander through the streets. The piazza in the centre of town is full of action and life. There is a large university here and groups of students are everywhere, passing the time in earnest conversation.

The 25th of April is a public holiday in Italy, but rather than celebrating Anzac Day as we do Australia, it is to celebrate liberation from fascism. It is a sunny, warm spring day so Giacinto, Madalena, myself and what feels like a thousand other Italians decide to visit St Francis Basilica in Assisi. The climb to the Basilica is torturous but as I enter the lower church I quickly forget my pain. The Basilica, both lower and upper churches, is the most spectacular I've ever seen. Its frescoes and elaborate decorations outshine all others and every possible centimetre of wall and ceiling is covered in the most rich, beautiful blues and reds. Intricate geometric designs encircle each fresco and cover any fragment of spare space. While other churches can seem overly elaborate with their use of coloured marble, gold, mosaic and stone, here is a picture of divine simplicity and the rawness of nature—geometric coloured tiles and stone on the floor, ornate but sombre wooden seats, a simple altar surrounded by soft lanterns and an unadorned cross hanging above the altar. The richness of colour on the ceilings and walls makes them seem as though they are covered in Persian rugs. I am not a religious person, but the design and beauty of the Basilica deeply moves me. It reflects perfectly what St Francis stood for.

Assisi itself looks over a large, flat valley of rich, green pasture and small hamlets and from the top of the old fort overlooking the city you can see Perugia and other Umbrian towns. There is such a lovely atmosphere in the streets on the day of our visit; large groups of young people sit in circles singing songs, children and what seems like busloads of scouts play games in the piazza, families walk together, everyone is enjoying the public holiday.

I discover it is worth exploring the winding, steep little roads of Assisi away from the Basilica too. Each house here is beautifully restored and cared for, and every street oozes charm. The brown of the stone and the window shutters, spring flowers on the windowsills and washing hanging out of windows soon takes me away on a journey to the past.

The trip to Assisi and back as a passenger in my cousin's car, however, is somewhat less restful. I have come to accept that high endorphin levels are quite the norm when travelling on Italian roads but somehow Madalena manages to sit relatively calmly in the front passenger seat as Giacinto zips around in his Alfa, colourful Italian invectives flying from his lips as he is frustrated by the chaos of Italian roads. I on the other hand end up with a stress-induced headache.

Italy is a country of contradictions. People frown if you don't put on a disposable plastic glove to handle the fruit and vegetable you wish to purchase, but happily throw rubbish out of their car windows. They are the most neatly groomed and tucked of people, yet cannot stay in one lane on a highway, preferring to drive in the centre just so they can honk to get you to move out of the way. They can be the most considerate of hosts, yet with complete disregard for others they will double-park and block you in. There are more cars than people in Italy and fewer parking spaces than people so you can imagine the daily struggles. Indeed Italy is really just one big car park and it seems you are free to park anywhere you please, just as long you put your hazard lights on. If you are blocked in simply honk your horn continuously for ten minutes and once the owner of the offending vehicle has finished their coffee and cigarette in the nearby bar they will come out and move their car. Simple.

Giacinto gives me lots of lessons on how to cope with driving here. Today as we are pulling out of his street to do a left turn the car coming towards us on our left has its indicator on. Giacinto explains, 'Now Angela, for you in Australia, you would say OK, we can go because she is going to turn and you could actually trust that she would turn. No; in Italy, you must hesitate as maybe she is one of the very small minority who indicate, maybe she's just forgotten and left her indicator on from a turn before, and maybe she is going to go straight. As the driver, we must go through every possible situation and then when we are sure she really, really is going to turn, then and only then can we go.' True to his warning, the woman drives straight on.

In Italy politics is a bit like driving. There is a lot of flash and a lot of bluff. In the past month I have been witnessing one of the craziest democracies in the world in action. It is election time and I am lucky enough to see all the candidates strut their stuff. Without understanding much of what they are saying I try making judgements about who might be best to lead Italy. The Italians, however, who love gold, silver, suntans and glitz, select a prime minister that epitomises all of this—a billionaire media magnate with show-pony arrogance. People cringe with embarrassment at comments he makes publicly, swear at the TV when he appears, laugh at his stupidity and shake their heads at his arrogance. And yet, it is him that they choose. Democracy in Italy remains a mystery to me.

I am taking my life in my hands once again as I climb into Giacinto's Alfa, but it is Sunday and Sundays in Fano are an opportunity to enjoy a drive through Le Marche, Umbria and Emilia-Romagna. We wind our way through the countryside, gently climbing Monte Petrano, a thousand-metre-high mountain in Le Marche. Unlike most mountains in the region the top of Monte Petrano in not peaked but a large, flat grassed plateau covered with yellow, white, purple and red wildflowers. I feel like Sister Maria from *The Sound of Music*; it is as if I am on the edge of the world. The view over Umbria and Le Marche is breathtaking. We lie flat on the spongy grass and soak up the gentle buzz of the insect life around us. As I lie on my stomach, my chin cupped in my hands, I look out across a sea of green and watch bees gently hopping from bloom to bloom. On the horizon fluffy white clouds bob along in the blue sky. I am floating above the earth on a blanket of grass.

As I roll over and the sun warms my chest my thoughts drift away to Sundays at home. Every Sunday evening without fail my family gathers for a meal of pasta together. It is always a simple meal but it is our tradition and one we hold dear. This ritual of sixteen people sharing pasta, prosciutto, salami, salad and fruit connects us all back to our Italian heritage. My father shines on Sunday nights, surrounded by his family, his grandchildren and his music.

I have been away three months now and I am starting to feel homesick. Yet I remind myself that this is a special time, a time to explore, to be me, to find me, and to discover a Valentino he can no longer describe. I Skype Mum and Dad. I am starting to laugh at the strong sound of her Australian accent—it makes me realise how long I've been away. Despite the progress I'm making with my Italian it is difficult to talk to Dad as he finds it nearly impossible now to speak on the phone. After I hang up a sadness and sense of loss washes over me. Dad's Alzheimer's is getting worse and I can hear in my mum's voice that she is finding it more difficult to care for him.

Polpette—Meatballs, two ways

Meatballs 1
   small handful of mince meat (beef or lamb)
   triple quantity (approx) grated fresh *pecorino*
      cheese to meat
   parsley
   garlic, minced
   eggs to bind
   olive oil
   carrot, chopped
   broad beans or peas
   salt and pepper

Mix the first five ingredients together well with your hands. Wet your hands and form small meatballs, the size of golf balls. Fry in olive oil until brown, then add some water and cover the pan. While the meatballs are simmering, add carrot, peas or broad beans and cook with the meatballs in the water. By the end of the cooking process they too will be tender yet caramelised. Continue cooking until all the water has evaporated and the meatballs get all sticky and scrumptious. Season with salt and pepper.

A good amount of eggs and cheese makes these very light and fluffy. For a meatier version, increase the ratio of meat to cheese.

Mop up the tasty pan juices with crusty bread.

Meatballs 2

500 g mince meat (pork and veal is a nice combination)
100 g breadcrumbs
1 small handful of currants
1 small handful of pine nuts
garlic
parsley
salt and pepper
1 egg
flour for dusting
olive oil
onions, chopped
broth/stock (about a cup)

Mix all ingredients except flour, onions and broth and bind with an egg. Make balls, dust them with flour and fry in oil. Add onions and cook for a few minutes. Add the broth and continue cooking gently until the sauce has thickened.

Cuckoo birds
and gondolas

As i wind my way north I arrive in Bergamo and my cousin Anna's little apartment becomes my new temporary home. Located in a courtyard that you enter through enormous old wooden gates along a cobblestone road, it is in a perfect location, close to everything, and absolutely gorgeous.

Bergamo is divided into two parts—*citta alta*, the high city, and *citta bassa*, the low city. Anna's apartment is on the cusp between the two. *Citta alta* is the old city state and rests on top of a hill, encircled by a large, forbidding wall. *Citta bassa* lies beneath. *Citta alta* has narrow, winding cobblestone roads that all weave their way towards the *duomo* at the centre of town. *Citta bassa* has wide boulevards, grand civic buildings and a shopping strip inlaid with marble mosaic. Bergamo is lovely, stylish and very northern; lots of polenta, cheese, Porsches, stiletto heels and designer dogs.

The weather has been delightful and the city is perfect for walking. I set off on one such scenic, local walk that starts in the hills behind *citta alta* and find myself following an ancient cobblestone road. The cobbles are not flat but rounded, popping up out of the ground in awkward yet lovely patterns. It's very hard to walk on, but thankfully there is a narrow flat path running beside it.

Bergamo is quite humid, the sky is again blue and the afternoon sun warm on my face and back. The path leads up a hill with farmland on either side. Fields give way to terraces as I climb higher. There are trees in every colour, shape and size: rich green oaks, trees covered in pink flowers, pine trees with what look like white Christmas candles decorating their branches, fruit trees and hedges. High above me at the crest of the hill I spy what looks like a fortress of tall walls and small windows made entirely of hedge. I later learn this is in fact a giant trap. The most famous dish in Bergamo is polenta with birds and this is the clever way they capture them. The birds fly through the small windows of the botanic fortress and get trapped inside where the hunters catch them ready for the kitchen.

For now I am blissfully unaware of their fate as I listen to the birds enjoying an afternoon of conversation, with a lone 'cuckoo, cuckoo, cuckoo' rising above the chorus. I hadn't heard a cuckoo before this trip, but now I hear them everywhere. Above the sounds of the breeze in the trees and the birds I hear the chimes of one of the many church bells in and around Bergamo. At all times of the day, I hear them ringing. In *citta alta*, the main bells in the piazza chime one hundred times at ten o'clock every night. In old times these chimes warned the locals that the city gates were closing and that they needed to finish their business or pleasure and enter the safety of the gates. Now they chime for nostalgia.

At the top of the Bergamo hills I pass an old monastery built six hundred years ago. Its walls are crumbling under the weight of its history and I try to imagine what life would have been like for the monks who once called it home, and what they would make of the villas sprinkled here now—large mansions with walled gates, manicured gardens and luxury cars in the driveway. Homes for the wealthy bankers who make Bergamo the city of plenty that it is.

I reach the top, footsore and with my face glowing in the afternoon heat. Looking down, I see the path winding its way down the valley, past the monastery, through the fields, and I smile.

Crostata
250 g plain flour
1 tsp baking powder
125 g butter at room temperature

100 g sugar
2 eggs
200 g jam
icing sugar

Put the flour and baking powder into a large bowl.
Use your fingertips to rub the butter into the flour,
then add the sugar. Add one beaten egg and mix
well. You may only need to add another egg yolk.
You don't want the dough too wet, but it will be
buttery and sticky. Add the second egg white if
needed. Don't overwork the dough.

Butter a flan dish. Using three-quarters of the pastry,
line the pan. Gently pat the dough into place over
the base and work the dough halfway up the sides
of the pan. Wrap the remaining pastry in cling wrap
and refrigerate both for 20 minutes.

Choose your favourite jam and spread about 200 g
over the pastry. Use the remaining pastry to make a
pattern on top. Bake in an oven at 180°C for 20–30
minutes; it is ready when the pastry has a nice colour
and pulls away from the sides.

Dust with icing sugar. Serve warm or cooled.

From Bergamo I head for Venice. On the train I finish
Sarah Dunant's *The Courtesan*, an epic story set in
the grand days of the Venetian empire and the perfect
antipasto to my visit. As I step out of the train station I

am blinded by the glistening Grand Canal. Riding in the *vaporetto* water taxi to my hotel as the day comes to a close, the colours of the buildings, gondolas and water are simply enchanting. Venice is truly an architectural miracle, a city built on water and mud.

There is just enough light left to see San Marco Square. I treat myself to a ridiculously priced glass of *prosecco* and watch the sun set over the Grand Canal. In the following days I walk through every quarter of the city, winding my way through the maze of tiny streets and managing not to get myself too lost. It's amazing how much you can see in two days if you avoid queuing at the museums. It is true that Venice is always crawling with tourists, but most stick to the same predictable paths and I don't have to wander too far before I find peace and quiet, and can hear the soft sound of lapping water, the call of gondola drivers, and witness the few Venetians left going about their business.

I fall in love with the islands of Venice. The main street of Murano is packed full of tourists ogling the glass the island is so famous for and that can be purchased in the many shops. But as I walk to the centre of the island where the locals live I once again find myself in a quiet, peaceful neighbourhood that moves with the beat of people living normal lives. It is Burano, however, that truly captures my heart. All the houses on this enchanting island are painted in vivid shades of purple, red, blue, green, pink and yellow and each is dressed with flowering pot plants. The island is a lively little centre of artisan workshops and fishermen, but it is most famous for its lace.

In Capoposta, my aunties all wove and embroidered their own pure linen. Traditionally they would use these skills to make their trousseau of bed linen, hand towels, nightshirts and underclothing. At home in Australia I have one hand-woven singlet that I adore, sewn and embroidered by my late aunt Giulietta, and I have promised myself I will return from Italy with a full linen service of tablecloth and matching napkins. I had planned to purchase this in Abruzzo but I am so struck by all the beautiful cloth and lace in Burano that I buy my set here. I cannot wait to use it.

On Mother's Day I go to Verona. It reminds me a lot of Florence, with the river winding its way through the town and the spectacular buildings. Rising up from the centre of Verona is the third most important Roman amphitheatre in existence. It is built from luscious pink marble and still functions as an opera theatre. I visit Juliet's balcony and climb the central bell tower for a magnificent view of the city—a sea of terracotta and pink marble.

On the day I arrive in Verona there happens to be a food festival on. Stalls from regions and provinces all over Italy are strewn with salamis, cheeses, olives and preserves. Then there is the bread. And there, brilliantly displayed, is my most favourite bread of all—ten-kilogram loaves of deeply rich Puglian bread. Puglian bread has a dark crust and a rich, golden and intensely velvety centre. Its robust flavour announces itself in your mouth and it is the perfect accompaniment to southern olive oil.

Sometimes I feel I can measure out my stay in Italy by the bread I consume. Bread is eaten at every meal here and it is an important part of the daily diet. Every area makes bread differently and the taste and textures vary throughout the country. My aunt buys bread by the kilo and is incredibly fussy about where her bread comes from and the type of flour used. The bread she buys comes in giant slabs or loaves. She holds a loaf to her chest and, using a huge bread knife, expertly slices towards herself, releasing chunks that she then frisbies to each person's place at the table.

For breakfast, my uncle and aunt eat thick slices of bread drizzled with olive oil and sprinkled with ground, dried capsicums. My brother Matt remembers on his first visit to Italy sharing breakfast with Zio Camillo, Dad's eldest brother. Our uncle held a fresh and extremely ripe summer tomato in his hand and gently squeezed it over the bread. He then drizzled on rich olive oil and sprinkled it all liberally with salt before washing down the lot with a glass of red wine.

I remember as a child my dad complaining when the bread Mum bought wasn't up to scratch. He really dislikes soft Australian bread and I remember him shaking a slice of bakery bread as he held it in his hand. As tiny pieces of dough fell to the table, he taught me that this was because the quality of the flour was poor and then told Mum never to buy it from that place again.

The pasta table that was my nonna's is actually a complete pasta- and bread-making cabinet. Directly under the large flat wooden top is a deep drawer that holds the flour and pasta-making equipment. My nonna would have a permanent yeast mother in that drawer. The ladies of the village would share the yeast mother so that a daily supply of homemade bread was always available. My nonna would open up the drawer, make the bread dough in a large bowl that sat in the drawer, then close the drawer to let the yeast do its work. In winter, to help the yeast, she would put hot coals in the cupboard that lies under the giant drawer.

When Dad was young, good-quality bread made with finely ground flour was reserved for special occasions. My nonna would make white bread and keep it in the bread drawer, away from the children and only to be brought out when visitors came. Mostly, they ate gritty cornbread. My dad and his sister Giulietta were close in age and friendship and one day they found a way to get into the bread cupboard. Zio Camillo, their older brother, was always quick to get his younger siblings in trouble so when he smelt sweet, white bread on their breath he told their mother. They were punished, but so determined were they to eat good bread that they figured out if they ate some cornbread immediately after, no one would be able to tell and so their crime spree continued.

Under the Tuscan clouds and finding George

I T IS MAY. I am almost halfway through my stay when my good friend Nat and her family arrive on holiday from Melbourne. We meet in Florence where we're to share a sunny and spacious apartment near Saint Ambrogio market. It is central enough to be able to walk everywhere but still has a slightly local feel to it. My heart thrills when I hear the doorbell ring and look out the window to see Nat and her burgeoning belly, her husband Mike, and their children Scarlett and Ginger smiling up at me over loads of luggage. It occurs to me how relaxing it will be to have close friends staying, to not feel like a guest and be on constant best behaviour. Talking nonstop with cups of tea in hand, I sometimes forget we're not in Melbourne.

But I am a proud host, showing off what language I have learnt and accompanying my friends on their walks through Florence. We go to the market most days and buy delectable goodies to cook at night. I set myself a challenge to cook a different pasta every day. We eat out too, especially pizza, and gelato, which the girls love.

Sagne pasta with asparagus

If you can't find *sagne*, you could use *fettucini* snapped into 3–4 cm lengths.

sagne pasta
1 bunch asparagus
salt
butter
parmesan
pepper
lemon zest

Cook *sagne* pasta in well-salted water. Meanwhile, chop a bunch of asparagus stalks into small pieces, leaving the heads whole. Cook the asparagus stems in a pan with a little water and salt until tender, then add the heads and cook briefly. Drain the water and add butter, then toss through cooked pasta, adding some pasta water and parmesan as you toss. Serve with lots of pepper. Lemon zest makes a nice addition to this recipe.

After five nights in Florence we embark on a road trip to the Tuscan countryside. We are quite a sight: three adults, two children, luggage, prams, a portacot and toys all crammed into a tiny Lancia.

Despite having lost our directions we somehow find our way to the country residence we've booked and breathe a sigh of relief as we pull up to our villa and the pool that is there waiting for us. It is a warm, humid afternoon and the kids are jumping out of their skins to get into the water. The complex is ideal. There are several apartments, each with their own private garden, and a couple of houses scattered about on the one property. We all share the pool. Our apartment has a glorious view and I spend many an evening sitting on the terrace watching the sun go down.

The next morning we head for Siena. The main piazza here is vast and strangely circular. Gently sloping towards the centre, it is like a lake of red stone surrounded by beautiful buildings. When we arrive it is full of people sitting on the pavement chatting, people-watching and eating lunch. We try to imagine the thump-thump of hooves and the electric atmosphere created by *Il Palio*, the historic horse race staged here every summer.

The weather unfortunately takes a turn for the worse and it is no longer warm enough to take advantage of our pool, so we head off in search of a large thermal spa complex not far from our village. We wait an eternity to be served and reluctantly agree to pay the equivalent of nearly eighty Australian dollars for a swim. Swimming caps are compulsory so we also pay extra for these. The halls are lined in clean, white lino with little numbered rooms on either side and the staff wear white uniforms and soft-soled shoes. The whole place has an eerie hospital-like feel.

A constant stream of overweight, middle-aged patrons, many with Eastern European accents, walk past clad in swimsuits and robes. Mike and I can't help but wonder what we are getting ourselves into but Scarlett is undeterred and jumps up and down, eager to get wet.

We are given our keys, one for Mike and another for us girls to go and change before making our way to the pool. We all dutifully put on our bathing caps. Nat is restricting her time in the hot pools because of her pregnancy and cannot stop laughing at us all swimming around in our hideous head gear. Ginger's is way too big, sitting on her head like a hankie from *Steptoe and Son*, and Mike has his handsomely pulled down over his ears. I have no doubt I am a vision of beauty too.

The pool is an adventure in itself with large, white buttons stationed all around the edge. Pressing them activates one or more of the various spa pumps, or so we think until I push one and a huge metal hose shoots a powerful squirt of water from the centre of the pool, almost decapitating an older woman as she swims by. As I get closer I am nearly knocked unconscious by the pressure. I'm still unsure of its therapeutic value. There are fountains, air blasts from the bottom and sides of the pool and a fast channel that either pushes you along or allows you to swim against it, should you dare. Exhausted and pruned-up after two hours of squirts, pumps and breaststroke, we bid farewell to our thermal spa and head for home.

We part company at Florence train station a few days later. Nat and her family are spending a couple of days in Rome while I'm heading north to Lecco. I am sad as I wave them off but content that I have shared this time with them. Two weeks with good friends has proved the perfect medicine for my homesickness.

Lecco is within the Como lake system, a lake town surrounded by rugged, jagged peaks. It is also the home of my good friend Tiziana and her family. I first met Tiziana when she came to Australia in her twenties for two extended stays with our family. She is an honorary member of our clan and has telephoned constantly since I arrived in Italy, eager to play host in her home town. Tiziana is married to Alberto and they have two gorgeous children, Edoardo and Claudia. I have arrived in time to celebrate Tiziana's fortieth birthday.

Despite the festivities I soon discover everyone is going a little mad in Lecco as they've had over a month of rain and there is no end in sight. All of Italy is now seemingly covered by a permanent rain cloud. My uncle's crops are spoiling, the kids have cabin fever and I start to forget what my blue-sky Italy looks like.

Lecco is not a tourist town like Como; instead it is a hub of industry, but it has its own beauty with its winding streets climbing up to the hills, its high-walled villas, tall trees, glistening lake and the falcons that glide majestically above. Lecco has a gorgeous but small central piazza that borders the lake. In the centre stands a grand church with a tall clock tower. The view from the piazza to the church with the mountain watching over it from behind is quite breathtaking.

The architecture is different here, more reflective of the fascist-era boom time for industry in the region. The stone is a grey/black colour, drawing from the colour of the mountains. In Italy all the cities and towns seem to reflect their environment. Assisi's rustic brown, Siena's red ochres, the hint of green stone of the Signora in Florence, the rich red marble in Bergamo, and of course the white marble in Rome.

From all around Lecco you see the mountains that surround the lake. The Como lake system itself is huge, shaped like an upside-down Y with Lecco at the bottom right tip and Como at the bottom left tip of the lake. It initially appears deep, dark and foreboding but when you get close the water is surprisingly clear and you can see large fish swimming around. Lecco has a series of torrents passing through it, winding their way from the mountains to the lake. Everywhere I go in the city I hear the rush of water reminding me that one is nearby. They are fast moving, cascading and energetic yet bring a peaceful calm to the urban surrounds. It is these torrents that I will remember most from my stay.

One day Tiziana, her friend Barbara and I go on a grand adventure in search of George Clooney. The morning newspaper headline read, '*George arrivato Laglio*', 'George has arrived at Laglio', the village where his villa is. They are all very proud of their illustrious neighbour here and there's been much discussion of late about his recent split from his very young girlfriend. Apparently the fruiterer who knows his butcher said it was because he didn't approve of her new silicone implants. I like him more and more.

We catch the ferry across to Menaggio and then head to the lovely lakeside village of Cadenabbia for a walk and lunch. For once the sun is out so we all have an extra bounce in our step. Each of the little villages surrounding the lake is quaint in its own right, many with elegant promenades planted with flowering beds and benches to sit and ponder life as you watch the boats gently float in the deep, deep water.

As we are sitting enjoying a beer on a hotel deck we all notice a sporty and very ritzy boat speed past. It is George, yes George, accompanied unfortunately by a couple of blonde girls. Well, we think it was him, but our possible sighting is enough to reignite our quest and we head off, winding our way along the sometimes perilous lakeside road in search of George's house in Laglio. We soon find it. It is of course the loveliest villa, with the highest and most secure gate.

Tiziana is keen to press the buzzer, labelled only 'villa' not 'Clooney', but chickens out at the last moment. It truly is a fortress and we will need our own ritzy speedboat if we are to get a better view.

As we ponder our options we hear the church bells chime two in the afternoon, time to pick the children up from school. Our little Hollywood star-spotting adventure is brought to an abrupt close by the mundanity of life and we wave goodbye to George, all secretly hoping we might run into him at the local bar or fruit shop another day.

Lake Como fish and risotto

I had this dish in Bellagio on Lake Como. It had been made with freshwater perch from the lake. If you're nowhere near Como, use flathead tails instead.

> 1 small onion, finely diced
> olive oil
> butter
> arborio rice (70–80 g per person)
> ½ glass white wine
> chicken stock
> grated parmesan cheese
> flathead tails
> breadcrumbs

Sauté the onion in oil and butter until glistening. Add arborio rice and stir so that all the rice gets coated with the oil and butter. The rice should glisten. Now add white wine and let it sizzle and evaporate. Meanwhile, ensure a pot of chicken stock is at boiling temperature. The stock should be the same temperature as the rice so that the cooking process is never interrupted. Add stock to the rice a ladle at a time, stirring regularly (always in one direction). Never drown the rice, but also don't let it get dry. Keep going until the rice is ready, which should take 20 minutes or so. It should be still bitey but not hard in the middle. At this point, turn off the heat. Add a knob of cold butter and a handful of grated parmesan cheese and stir vigorously. This will give the risotto its final creamy and luminous touch. Lightly coat fish in breadcrumbs and cook in a little butter. Serve on top of the plain risotto.

I've booked a spot to see Leonardo da Vinci's *Last Supper* in Milan on 24 June. I've just finished reading another fantastic historical novel, *Leonardo's Swans*, by Karen Essex. It is set in the period when da Vinci was under the patronage of the Duke of Milan and has made his influence on the Milan landscape so much more vivid and alive for me, especially when I see the *navigli*, the canals shaped by da Vinci's brilliant mind. It has long been my habit to read novels set in the cities I'm visiting. I arrived in Lecco after my holiday with

Nat to find an English copy of *I Promessi Sposi* (*The Bethrothed*) by Alessandro Manzoni on my bed. This is Italy's *Romeo and Juliet*, set in Lecco and written a couple of hundred years ago by Manzoni, who grew up there. I have already set aside the *Inspector Moltalbano* series by Andrea Camilleri for my trip to Sicily.

I call home again. This time Dad manages through all his language difficulties to ask me the same question he has asked whenever he's been able: 'When are you coming home?' My heart breaks.

Summer

Pink sunsets
and fields of hay

B EFORE RETURNING SOUTH to Abruzzo, I take
a detour to Liguria to see the Cinque Terre,
five isolated villages clinging to the Ligurian coast.
The villages are linked by a train line and a walking
track and it is a favourite place for walkers and lovers
of intimate Italian village life. Between each village
vineyards and crops cling precariously to the steeply
terraced earth. While it appears idyllic and serene I can
only imagine how brutal, isolated and hard the work
to cultivate this land must be.

I base myself in Monterosso, the first of the five
villages, for five nights, enough time to enjoy the beach
and explore the villages and coastline. Monterosso has
long beaches and the most restaurants and shops of the
five villages that make up the Cinque Terre. On my

first day I hire an umbrella and a lounge, which comes with a private beach, a lifeguard, beautifully clean toilets, showers and a bar. For this I pay fifteen euros for the day. For a travel-weary girl suffering from heat rash and in need of some pampering it is worth every penny and I decide to extend my reserved umbrella oasis by another day.

By eight in the evening the sun is hidden behind the hills but its rays still cast a glow across the land and as I look out at the sea it glistens silver. Yachts bob and make contrasting shadows against the darkening sky. The beach is lined with coloured umbrellas, folded now but still standing at attention like terracotta warriors preparing for the onslaught of beach-goers tomorrow. As I look east down the coast each of the other four villages of the Cinque Terre glows pink in the fading light.

In search of a relaxing drink to end my day I choose an appealing *enoteca*, a wine bar, under a grand old tree dotted with fairy lights. I settle in and work my way through a tasting of four local wines. The first is crisp and peachy, the second as clean as snow, the third like caramel and the last and oldest reminds me of a good *Taleggio* cheese. Next to the bar are faded pink houses covered with vivid purple flowers. A parade of tourists and locals passes by, the tourists looking up while quietly talking to each other, the locals looking straight ahead unless saluting and yelling messages to people on the balconies above. The blend of tourism and local life is very apparent here. Everywhere I go I see fishermen hauling their catch up the steps, people having loud conversations across balconies and nonnas babysitting their grandchildren.

The next day I wander from Vernazza's train station down a winding paved street to the piazza in the second village along the Cinque Terre's rocky shore. Every house has sheets and clothes hanging from the window. Fishing boats sit in front of these houses, having been pushed up from the dock after a hard day's work. Everywhere old ladies and idle men sit passing the time as they watch the tourists go by. At the piazza bright red and pink buildings line the circumference and a quaint church watches over the water as if ensuring good fortune and safe return to the fishermen who leave. The water sparkles as I drink my spritz aperitif.

Later that evening while eating pizza outside a restaurant I notice an old lady with a walking stick slowly making her way down the path, while being overtaken by a succession of impatient young people. When she arrives at the *pizzeria* she stands at the door and screams out something to the lady running the place before plonking herself on a bench outside. Within minutes, a waiter appears with two salami sandwiches and a glass of red wine. When she has finished, she gets up, walks to the *pizzeria* door and screams, '*Grazie.*' All the staff respond good night in chorus, '*Buona sera, Silvia.*' She then slowly waddles her way back up the winding steps to her house.

There are many dishes that are particular to Liguria and I am working my way through quite a few. Ligurians eat a lot of anchovies, served in many different ways. Despite my aversion to seafood the atmosphere of fishing boats, fishermen and the salt air entices me to try as much of the local produce as I can. My favourite of the Ligurian anchovy dishes is fresh fillets marinated in lemon juice; tangy morsels from the sea. The preferred pasta here is *trofie* served with pesto. *Trofie* pasta is shaped like little twisted worms. Coated with the lusciousness of fresh basil pesto, this dish is quite simply Liguria on a plate. For me though, the most unique dish of the region is pasta with walnut sauce. This rich, creamy and hearty meal is so different from the tomato-based pastas of Abruzzo. Liguria is also well known for its tiny brown olives, rich in flavour yet light on flesh; a little bowl accompanying an aperitif while watching the sun set is a perfect end to any day.

Pesto pasta

Once you make pesto a couple of times, you will learn that you don't need to be too precise with the ingredients. Most recipes have more garlic, but I find it too pungent. I have even made it with no garlic, which is quite refreshing. If you don't have *pecorino* cheese, just use parmesan. The traditional shape of pasta for pesto is *trofie*, which can be bit hard to find. You can substitute any shape really.

½ clove of garlic
pinch of salt
1 cup basil leaves
1 tbsp pine nuts
4 tbsp olive oil (approx)
1–2 tbsp grated *pecorino*
1–2 tbsp grated parmesan
pasta

Place the garlic and a pinch of salt in a mortar and grind with the pestle. Add the basil leaves and continue pounding until the leaves have broken up. Add the pine nuts and continue pounding until smooth. Gradually add the olive oil and mix into a silky paste. Stir in the cheeses.

Boil pasta in salted water. Drain pasta, reserving some of the water. Toss the pesto gently through the pasta, adding some pasta water to enhance the creaminess.

This pesto is also delicious served with boiled potatoes and green beans.

As much as I have loved my time in the Cinque Terre I am excited to get back to Capoposta. I return on 4 July, Mum and Dad's wedding anniversary. It has been nearly three months since I left for my travels in the north and I have become desperate to feel at home again, to see everyone and eat Abruzzese once more.

I arrive in the midst of harvesting season. It is hot and humid but a pleasant breeze makes it more comfortable and everywhere tractors are working over-time cutting and rolling hay and harvesting the wheat. I hear the chug chug of their engines all day and late into the night.

I go for a ride on one of these tractors to see the large harvester in action and for a tour of the land that originally belonged to my grandfather and his brothers, now split up into the tiny inherited plots that make the Abruzzo countryside the amazing patchwork that it is. We go to the olive grove planted by my Nonno, which I've already been told I will be harvesting in November, and see the lovely, knotty old trunks with their branches stretching out for sunlight. The leaves are a beautiful soft green and the trees are covered in buds awaiting the summer. I have a deep sense of belonging standing amongst these trees. In my mind's eye I see my grandfather and grandmother resting in their shade, I see my dad as a boy playing and working here and I see the efforts of their toil.

Zio Alberto stands proudly as he shows me the land, describing who has what, who inherited what, and when vines and olives were planted. This is the heart of Di Sciascio land. Early last century my grandfather and his brothers took an adventurous journey to the other side of the world. They worked incredibly hard, sweat-ing in hot furnaces to get the money to buy the land where I now stand. As I watch the huge *trebbia*, the harvester, reap the wheat so easily, my uncle tells me of the backbreaking work of the past when they harvested by hand, using a sickle and then threshing the wheat before transporting the produce by horse and cart. He sighs at the changes time has brought, but cannot help but be relieved by the presence of the machines.

My uncle has already harvested the majority of his wheat. Most goes straight to the co-op, but a year's worth of chicken feed is now stored in the loft next to my bedroom. What's left of the cut hay stands short in the earth, leaning in all directions to create an illusion like water flowing, while on top sit the large balls of prepared hay ready for the stables. My uncle and all the men-folk now have deep, leathery tans on their forearms, face and the V of their shirt-fronts, evidence of long, hot hours spent working in the fields. The grapevines are rich with big bunches of small green grapes now and the air smells of cut grass.

Zia Rosaria's magnificent summer vegetable garden is a sight to behold, complete with tomatoes, beans, peppers, potatoes, corn, onions, garlic, carrots, zucchini, melons, lettuce, silverbeet and cucumbers. The potatoes will be stored in the attic for use all year, as will the garlic and onions. Today I watch my aunt tie the garlic into plaits ready for hanging.

Pasta with green beans, potato and tomato
   bucatini pasta
   tomato pulp
   garlic

parsley
celery leaves
potatoes
fresh herbs to flavour
green beans

Snap *bucatini* into 5 cm lengths. Cook until *al dente* in well-salted water. Meanwhile, prepare a plain tomato sauce with tomato pulp, garlic, parsley and celery leaves. In a separate pot, boil a couple of potatoes cut into cubes. My aunt puts herbs in the water to flavour the potato. Cut beans into the same lengths as the pasta and boil separately. Cook well, as the beans should be the same consistency as the *al dente* pasta. When the pasta is ready, toss all ingredients together. You can add fresh parsley too.

I am getting up earlier and earlier, woken by the sun, the heat and some incredibly noisy roosters. My aunt feels guilty about her rooster and says that tomorrow it may be heading for the chop. Poor thing; I feel that with the mere mention of chickens I am issuing a death sentence.

When I was growing up, my father always rose early. He was out of the house before most of the family had risen and used to scold me for sleeping in and wasting the day. He especially hated it when I came home at all hours after having been out clubbing. I remember coming up the driveway early one morning just as he was leaving. We passed without speaking. I was ashamed and he was shamed. He didn't speak to me for two days.

When Zio Alberto speaks of my father when he was younger he tells many stories of Dad's late nights, how he would walk for miles to go to parties in other villages and would try to sneak home early in the morning without his father noticing. Sometimes he got caught and bore the wrath of my grandfather's notorious temper; other times he got away with it. Often Dad would find a good place in the corn field to fall asleep, hidden from his father who thought he was busy working. My uncle remembers dragging Dad through a crop by his feet and Dad remaining fast asleep. In all the years that Dad lectured us kids about staying out all night he never once mentioned that he used to do the same.

Maria Chiara and I go to the top of Maiella Mountain to take a photo in the same place that I took one back in January when everything was covered in snow. It is so peaceful, green, clean and untouched; it is as though I am standing on top of the world. From my uncle's house I can see the place where I stood that day and it seems a heaven away.

The Abruzzo mountains are magnificent, green and rocky with stone so white it shines in the sunlight. The villages in the mountains are all made of this beautiful white stone and the large treeless plains and valleys are perfect for grazing. It is this that the Abruzzo mountains are famous for, an ancient trail for shepherds called the *Transumanza*. For centuries shepherds have been herding their flocks along this path through the mountains in accordance with the seasons.

Scanno is one of the more beautiful villages along the *Transumanza* and I am lucky enough to be here for a religious festival. The whole town is involved in the celebration. The old women are dressed in traditional Scanno clothing—long skirts with heavily detailed pleating—and the festival is exactly what I imagine a small-town religious parade to be. A solemn priest carrying a large cross leads a parade of locals dressed in beautiful, colourful outfits and looking like grown-up altar boys; all the children are wearing white and a giant statue of the Madonna is lifted through the winding streets; and accompanying them all is a slightly out-of-tune band. Locals line the streets and balconies observing the goings on. It is gaudy, over-the-top, ritualistic, steeped in history and sombre all at once. Floating above, the smell of lamb *sugo* wafts out of every window, gently simmering in preparation for lunch. This is my Italy.

I delight in the food of the season; cucumber and fresh tomato, young capsicum salad and pasta *fagioli* made with borlotti beans picked from the garden. One day I ask Zia Rosaria why some of the chickens have no feathers on their necks. She explains that it is just the way with this breed and that they are great for barbecue. The next morning she rises early, kills, plucks and cleans one of them, builds a fire despite the summer heat and slowly lets it barbecue over the coals. She serves it for lunch, just so I can experience their flavour. It is the most incredible chicken I have ever eaten.

Chicken—Three ways

The meat of my aunt's chickens is dark, has rich yellow fat and is juicy and full of flavour. It is home grown, free range and organic. I will never eat mass-produced chicken again.

Pollo sotto il coppo

Cooked under a cover in a wood fire

A *coppo* is a large steel lid with tall sides that fits comfortably over a baking dish (a bit like a hat), which in turn sits in the base of a wood fire. It has a large steel handle on top and is very similar to a camp oven.

> fresh free-range organic chicken
> garlic
> salt
> ground coriander seeds
> fennel seeds
> fresh herbs
> olive oil
> potato

Marinate the chicken in garlic, salt, ground coriander seeds, some fennel seeds and lots of herbs. It is best left overnight if you have the time.

Prepare a fire so that it is hot with coals.

Par cook chicken in a little oil, herbs, garlic and a little water on the stove top for approximately 30 minutes. (This step is optional.) Add pieces of potato.

Sweep the fire coals to form a circle the size of the *coppo*. Put the chicken pan on the hot hearth. Cover with the *coppo* and place hot coals all over the top of it. Sweep the rest of the hot coals around the edge of the *coppo*. Put any logs or larger pieces of wood from the fire on top of the *coppo* and ensure they are alight. Add more bracken to the top and light if necessary. To check the meat, take off the logs and place to the side of the fire. Use fire tongs to lift the *coppo* by the handle and place to the side. You can now check the meat, turn it or add other ingredients, then return the *coppo* and the logs and ensure the coals are snug around the edges again.

Cook under the *coppo* for 45 minutes to an hour.

This recipe is suitable for rabbit too.

Roast chicken

Marinate chicken pieces as for the *sotto il coppo* recipe and place in a roasting dish with some of the herbs and garlic. Add some potato pieces, oil and a bit of water and roast until all juicy and sticky. Plenty of bay leaf is good in this recipe.

Barbecued chicken

Marinate chicken in garlic, salt, ground coriander
and herbs. Butterfly the chicken by cutting along
the spine, sandwich it into a doubled-sided wire
rack and barbecue over the hot coals of a wood fire.
Don't have the chicken too close to the coals; let
it cook slowly and it will keep its juices. Turn the
chicken frequently and baste with oil using a sprig of
rosemary. This dish has a really smoky flavour. You
can use the same method for rabbit.

Now that it is summer I take my walks earlier to avoid
the heat and people have been asking my uncle where
the 'walking girl from Australia' has gone. Today I am
heading for Ascigno to visit the couple I met months
ago in their lovely vegetable garden. The signora is
pleased to see me and as I am red-faced, hot and sweaty
she sits me down for a cool drink and the obligatory
piece of cake. She notes that my Italian is better, and
this alone makes the journey worth it.

Lentils, love and L'Aquila

M Y BEDROOM SITS directly above the stable. At night I can hear the movement of cows and in the morning I hear my uncle and aunt talking to them as they milk. One evening, I notice a little more noise than usual. My aunt hears it too and wakes everyone to say that the cow is ready to give birth. Unexpectedly for all, not one but two calves enter the world that night. I have tears in my eyes and watch in sheer wonder as my aunt and uncle pull out two beautiful black baby cows. Zio Alberto looks at me with pride, his arm in a cow's vagina right up to his shoulder. It is messy and bizarre and fantastic.

The cattle of Capoposta provide milk for cheese, fertiliser for the fields, veal meat and in times gone by, warmth on a winter's evening. Cheese is made almost daily here. It is mostly eaten fresh, but the older cheeses have a pepperiness and enhanced saltiness to them. It is grated in meatballs and other savoury dishes, eaten as an *antipasto*, used as filling for sweet pastries, or sliced and fried in a pan. Pan-fried, it squeaks in your mouth like haloumi and is a delicious light meal. Zia Rosaria makes her cheese using the intuition and instinct of someone who has been doing this nearly every day for decades. As she transforms milk into discs of beautiful cheese, I am mesmerised by the rhythm of her labour, and savour the prospect of sharing the fruits of it.

As well as the one road in Capoposta, there is an endless maze of tractor paths winding their way through the fields and groves. I decide to walk along one that goes to my grandfather's olives, following it to the end. It is a warm day and a long way but well worth it. Everywhere there is silence and calm. As the wind rustles through the trees I close my eyes and I'm transported to my favourite beach in Australia, Jan Juc; the sounds are just the same.

The path is isolated but unlike back home I don't feel the same urgency to be constantly on the lookout for snakes. I follow it down the valley to a small wood with a little creek but water is covering the path so I turn back. When I arrive home puffed and hot I tell Zio Alberto and cousin Mattia where I have been.

They have a little chuckle and ask if I came across any snakes. Then my uncle gets serious. 'You should be careful walking down there, there are *cinghiale*.' *Cinghiale*. Wild boar. I have visions of being chased by a beast like the one from the horrific Australian movie *Razorback*. I can almost hear the squeals and my screams, and my fears become even worse when I find out that wild boars come up into Zia Rosaria's garden and at times have eaten all of her corn.

While I may be terrified at the thought of coming face to face with a wild boar, eating them is quite a different matter. I have got quite accustomed to seeing a boar head out the front of a butcher or cured meat shop; and I've had some lovely wild boar stews and sausages. Either caught by hunters or farmed in large, fenced-in properties where the boar are left to roam freely as in the wild, the meat is rich and dark and I think best in a slow-cooked *ragu*.

One day my two cousins Rino and Basilio decide to take me on an outing. We are going to the Grotto Cavallone, a deep cave high in the Maiella Mountain. Rino is an electrician and maintains the chairlift, tiny, one-person cages that take us to the summit, but ironically—and to my secret relief—when we arrive it is out of order. Instead we take Rino's four-wheel drive up the incredibly steep and slippery service road. I thought I had become hardened to Italian driving but as the road zigs and zags its way up the mountain at a very steep gradient on a path made solely of large slippery mountain stones, I truly believe my days are at an end.

My relief at reaching the top turns to despair when I see what seems like a thousand steps leading up to the entrance of the cave. The boys are experienced mountain climbers and set off effortlessly with me trailing behind, my legs like rubber, my hair limp with sweat and my face bright red. When we get inside the cave the chilly atmosphere cools me immediately. Scrawled on the walls are the names of the hundreds of people who hid here during the war. They are a sobering and eerie sight, these autographs, village names and dates written in coal, a permanent record of a terrible plight. There are names from Chieti and Lanciano, cities miles from here, and we find a Di Sciascio from Guardiagrele too.

The evenings are long in summer and perfect for social gatherings. Giacinto comes home to Abruzzo every summer and one night I accompany him and his family to Casoli for a *cac'e ove* festival. *Cac'e ove*, cheese and egg balls, are an Abruzzese staple. The main street is closed and filled with trestle tables. The ladies of the town volunteered their time over the last four days to make thousands of these cheese balls in tomato *sugo*, which are sold to the public to raise money for the church youth activity centre. It is a lovely night and the first time I have eaten these treats. I will never forget it: an evening of music, dancing, lots of eating and of course what Italians like to do most—talking.

Cac' e ove (Cacio e uova)
Cheese and egg balls in tomato sauce

300 g grated fresh *pecorino* cheese (not aged—
   sometimes called *pecorino bambino* in Australia)
200 g fresh breadcrumbs
6 eggs
parsley, finely chopped
salt and pepper

Mix all ingredients together and make small balls the
size of golf balls. Fry in a pan with oil until browned.
Drain on kitchen paper then add to a good basic
tomato sauce (see tomato *sugo* recipe).

A note on the cheese. Fresh *pecorino* can be difficult
to grate. One way to solve this is to unwrap the
cheese and leave it in the fridge to dry out for a
couple of days before you need it. Alternatively,
replace the cheese with hard cheese such as *grana
padana, parmigiana* or aged *pecorino*. I have also
tried this recipe with 150 g fresh *pecorino* and 150 g
grana padana and it was delicious.

I am out walking one hot summer's day when I pass
an old lady in front of her house mincing tomatoes
under the shade of a tree. It is tomato season. Every

vegetable patch is laden with rows and rows of tomato vines decorated like Christmas trees with bright red, ripe fruit. Two hours later I pass her house again. By now she is standing next to a huge pot, stoking a fire beneath. I've seen these pots before; they are about a metre in diameter and are used for sterilising and preserving tomato pulp. This one is sitting in a clearing near the house and the old lady is tending it carefully. She is dressed like many old women here— dark clothes covered with an overdress that serves as an apron, and a head scarf on her head. As I pass I say hello and she calls me over. Seeing me with water bottle in hand, walking on the road towards nowhere, she asks the same questions I always get asked—where have you been and where are you going? I explain that I am walking to Capoposta and that I am Valentino's daughter. I am no surprise to her; she has heard of the Australian girl and knows all about me. She then surprises me by announcing that her younger sister was in love with my dad when they were young. She is very pleased to hear that he now has six children. As I walk home I am smiling, having discovered another chapter of my dad's past.

I relay the story to my uncle and aunt and they proceed to tell me all about the beautiful girl who was once in love with my dad.

My dad has a very old photo album that contains all his photos of family and bachelor life. It also holds the remains of a loose-leaf collection of papers with notes in my father's handwriting: the diary he wrote while on his journey across the seas to Australia. On the last page of the album he has written the names and birthdates of his children as we were born. I love this book. Some years ago Mum made copies of the photos and gave each of her children a precious album explaining our Italian family tree, a translation of Dad's diary, a history of his work and his life after he migrated to Australia and, of course, all the old photos of Italy and Dad. In the original, though, way in the back, there is a small sepia picture of a girl. She is attractive and serious and has rich curls styled in the fashion of the 1940s. When I ask Dad who the girl is he always replies, 'Just a girl from Italy.' I think of this picture now. Could that lady's sister be the girl in the photo?

I ask Zio Alberto. He looks at my aunt. 'Hmmm, it could be. But maybe it's Bambina from Colle Bianco, or Antonietta from Colle Bianco.' Just how many girls were in love with my dad? In the words of my aunt, 'Valentino was a beautiful man when he was young, a bit short, but beautiful, and he played the accordion.' Seems all girls love a musician. After a few questions to my mum and a little more digging, I finally discover who the mystery girl is.

Just a girl from Italy? The truth is that she was not just a girl; she was potentially *the* girl for Dad. It is Bambina and she and Valentino had been in love, communicating with each other through secret letters passed by hand between their villages. Dad's parents weren't happy with the match. Her family didn't have any land and therefore she was not suitable. I shudder when I think of this, that land and dowry were more important than the happiness of a child. Bambina's father was away working in Argentina so when the prospect of marrying my father was scuttled she decided to accompany her mother and join him there. On the day of her departure she and her mother had to walk past the fountain to get the bus. Dad, accompanied by his best friend, waited at the fountain. It was there in that public space that they bid each other a very private farewell. My father was inconsolable and his friend recalls that it was one of the most emotional sights he has witnessed. It was the hopelessness of this situation that sealed my dad's decision to leave for Australia.

While the thought of my dad having girlfriends tickles me and I feel sad for the loss of his first love, the reality is that romance was a far more difficult business then. Unmarried girls were not able to talk to unmarried boys without a chaperone; there were no private moments and absolutely no touching. They couldn't even dance. Girls could dance with other girls, their fathers, brothers or uncles, but definitely not with single boys. My uncle did not have his first private conversation with my aunt until after they were married. Talking about this with my cousin Anna, she tells me it was lucky for Valentino and Bambina that they could write to one another. Her mother, my dad's sister Giulietta, was illiterate. It was not seen as necessary to educate girls at that time. In just one generation, the world of women in Italy has completely changed.

I take my uncle's Fiat Panda along the highway for the thirty-minute drive to Fossacesia Beach. Unlike the golden sandy beaches of Australia, Fossacesia is covered in large white stones the size of your palm. It's made up of private beaches along with patches of free beach and everyone uses umbrellas without fear of them flying away as there is only ever a gentle breeze here. I arrive armed with an umbrella, a rolled up piece of foam to lie on and a sun chair and set myself up for a glorious day. The water is quite salty and I can actually float on my back with my head resting on my arms and have a snooze without fear of drowning. I suspect it is this high salt content that explains why I see people rinsing themselves under the showers after a swim, often then putting on a second pair of bathers. Some people's methods for doing so in public are quite ingenious. One couple has devised a system similar to a giant burqua. They hop under it with just the top of their heads poking out, change in the privacy of this one-man, homemade tent, then lie on their sun chairs for their next hour of sunbaking.

The water is clean and warm, flat and peaceful; it is like swimming in a giant pool. Beaches are rated by cleanliness in Italy and many of the Abruzzo beaches are classified 'Blue Flag', the cleanest. Except for me, everyone wears a bikini, even old ladies. In a nation obsessed with beauty and style I love how these rules don't apply the moment you arrive at the seaside. People of all shapes and sizes enjoy the beach as a social event and you can hear the chatter as people gossip their way through the day.

By twelve o'clock, most people have packed up and headed home for lunch and siesta before returning at about four. It is a take on beach life that I am growing to love. Arriving by 8.30 am, I enjoy a couple of long swims, sit in the sun without fear of frying, read my book under my umbrella and then return home for a three-course lunch. All very civilised.

I leave my beachside idyll to return to Fano, in Le Marche. I am staying with my cousin Giacinto again and catching up with my brother Simon, who is here with the Australian 4-way skydiving team. They are on a training camp before heading to France for the world championships. It is wonderful seeing him and hearing all those Australian accents. The airport where they train is just near my cousin's house and as we sit talking in the backyard we can hear the ascent of the plane each time the team does a practice jump. If we look in the right place, we can even see them parachuting down. Sunday is a rest day so my cousin invites the team to his house for a six-course lunch. They are a little overwhelmed by the volume of food and hospitality but Madalena's Abruzzese cooking goes down well, as does her homemade *limoncello*.

Viewing these Australian blokes through the eyes of my cousins I catch a glimpse of what they see in me and my brothers. I have for six months been absorbed in Italian life and now feel a part of it, even though some aspects still frustrate me. Watching the boys, I realise how different I still am from my Italian family. At our best Australians are jovial, relaxed (so relaxed we take our shoes off, which is an absolute no-no in Italy), open, sarcastic, accepting, multicultural, adventurous and tolerant. We take people for who they are and don't pretend to be something we aren't. We have confidence, yet we are happy to make fun of ourselves and we don't preoccupy ourselves worrying what other people think of us.

I think for Italians, this can be a little confronting. It is not that Italians are none of these things but if I were to describe the Italian character I would say they are loyal, have a strong sense of the aesthetic, that they are respectful yet irreverent, serious, defined by their past, hardworking, steadfast and family focused. Maybe this list will grow by the time I leave. As I read it over I realise I have just described my dad.

I have a big map of Abruzzo and each time I visit a village or town I circle it. Looking at this map I realise there is a whole section of Abruzzo I haven't seen, the province of L'Aquila. As my cousins Maria Chiara and

Anna are on holidays for the summer, we decide to take a trip. We plan the villages we want to see and, armed with a road map and guide book, set off.

Our first stop is Capestrano, a quaint village with a quaint piazza. Above the piazza and the town is an old castle that has now been restored and is used by the council as offices. At the opposite end of the piazza stands the town church and across from this, painted on the wall of a neighbouring building, is an old faded fascist propaganda slogan that reads, '*L'Italia fascista può, se sarà necessario portare oltre il suo tricolore, abbassarlo mai.*' Basically this translates as, 'Fascist Italy may, if it is necessary to carry further its flag, never lower it.' The slogan itself is not particularly important, indeed it's a bit confusing, but it does remind me of a part of Italian history that has helped shape our family.

Fascism had a defining effect on my father. His father was openly anti-fascist, which didn't help his family when the municipality was under fascist control. I remember in the early eighties my little brother coming home with a flat-top haircut that was all the rage at the time. When he saw it Dad was very upset. It reminded him of his childhood and the regime. That haircut was more than fashion to him; it was a symbol of right-wing power and the destruction of peace in Italy. My father used to lecture me about keeping my political beliefs to myself. He said that I could believe what I wanted but to openly display my convictions meant that our family would be labelled with those convictions, as his family was when his father was openly critical of fascism. While I was at university studying politics I had all the fervour and social consciousness of a twenty-something socialist but I never joined a party, never participated in university politics and never displayed my political beliefs too openly—the words of my father were a constant in my mind.

The next village we visit is Castel del Monte and we arrive right in the middle of their feast day. After squeezing our way into a park on a narrow street with a very steep incline, we follow the sounds of music to the centre of town. Italy is alive with festivals in the summer. Each town has a patron saint that the main church is usually named after and there is always a festival held in their honour. The town is fitted out with decorative lights, the square is crammed with market stalls, and the church holds its biggest mass of the year and is filled to capacity. There is music, dancing, fireworks, and often a parade to and from the church. Everyone dresses in their finest and has a wonderful time. The *festa* at Castel del Monte is no different. We follow the crowd to and from the church, check out the market and have a drink at the central bar before heading off.

By now we are in the middle of the Gran Sasso National Park. Most of Abruzzo is located in one of the four national parks that dominate the landscape here. I am eager to see this part of Abruzzo, especially *Campo Imperatore*, the Tibet of Europe. We wind our way along the scenic mountain road. What makes this part of Abruzzo so wonderful and different from Casoli is its remoteness. As the nickname implies, it is barren, with small clusters of houses forming mountain villages. There are no farmhouses in between. It is remote, rugged, wild and very, very cold in winter. Most of the villages are as they were five hundred years ago, with their populations dwindling. It's a tough existence and not one that people of my generation have hung around for. But gradually this is changing as city folk discover these villages; slowly buildings are being restored and life is starting to return in the form of tourism. It astounds me how few tourists visit Abruzzo but when I mention this, my cousins hush me, saying, 'Ssshhhh, don't tell anyone how beautiful it is here. We don't want it to get like Tuscany, Umbria and Le Marche.'

The *Campo Imperatore* is a huge plain set high in the middle of the mountains. From here all the Abruzzo mountains are visible. It's hot and dry now, no snow caps, just grassy plains, white rocky terrain and stony grey mountain peaks. Every now and then we see a flock of sheep with a deeply tanned shepherd watching over them, or a herd of cattle with large bells hanging around their necks. These animals are revered here for their mountain cheese, especially *pecorino*. The landscape, however, is barren and ominous.

We twist and turn back down the mountain to San Stefano di Sessanio. This is a spectacular village with virtually no modern buildings. We stop here to savour the local produce of *Campo Imperatore*—tiny melt-in-your-mouth lentils, legumes, *pecorino*, saffron, almonds and lamb. Our soup arrives, a terracotta bowl filled with the tiny brown lentils swimming in a broth and glistening with a serious swig of olive oil. It is served with croutons and the most important condiment, grated *pecorino piccante* (old and sharp). The texture of the broth and the croutons are a divine combination but for me, it's the addition of the *pecorino* that makes this dish perfect.

We try other food typical to the area on our journey: lamb cooked in loads of herbs and Trebbiano wine, rabbit cooked with pancetta and almonds, saffron risotto, local cheeses, and baked *scamorza* cheese. The Abruzzese, like all Italians, love their food. People travel for miles simply for a dish made in a particular town, just as we did for the lentil soup. As we are driving across the deserted plain we see in the distance a gathering of cars. Here, literally in the middle of nowhere, is a butcher serving one of the most aromatic of all Abruzzo dishes—*arrosticini*. Basically, it is mountain mutton pieces alternated with chunks of fat on skewers then barbecued over piping hot coals on specially made iron barbecues. I remember Dad made one of these barbecues when I was young. Here at maybe the most isolated picnic ground in the world, people buy the meat already prepared then sit at large picnic tables with small *arrosticini* barbecues and cook their own meat treats in the company of friends, surrounded by mountain peaks.

Pasta con cece
Pasta with chickpeas

This dish is best served with short pasta, perhaps *penne*, snapped *buccatini*, shells or *farfalle*.

> pasta
> chickpeas
> olive oil
> garlic clove
> dried capsicum skins or paprika
> parsley
> hard cheese, grated

Cook pasta until *al dente* in water that has been salted well.

Prepare chickpeas as required (if dry, soak overnight and boil; if canned, drain and rinse).

In a pan, heat some oil with a smashed garlic clove to infuse. Remove the garlic and add crushed dried capsicum skins (or you can use paprika) and toss along with the chickpeas and pasta. You may need to add a spoon or two of pasta water. Add parsley and serve with cheese.

Our next stop, Castelvecchio Calvisio, is a medieval fortified village. It has an orthogonal layout with a main narrow path through the middle and side lanes leading out to the walls. These narrow lanes are filled with arches and external stairs that seem to defy gravity and look positively perilous for those who need to use them. This is my favourite destination in the L'Aquila province. We are the only people wandering around its laneways and it is completely quiet. Many buildings are now abandoned but occasionally we see signs of life: an old lady knitting outside her front door, flowering pot plants outside a window decorated with hand-woven and embroidered linen curtains, a boy cycling home, or the smell of a pasta sauce simmering. As we break through the tiny exits in the town walls we are struck by the view of our last destination for the day—Rocca Calascio.

Rocca Calascio is a castle built on a seemingly inaccessible cliff high in the mountains. It is visible from most vantage points in the *Campo Imperatore*. It was possessed by the Medicis in the late Middle Ages (as were many of the other villages we visited), as its position helped control the valuable ancient sheep migration tracks. We make our way slowly up the narrow mountain road to the castle. Just below the castle there is a collection of buildings that have been abandoned. A few years ago people started the painstaking job of restoring these houses and it's here that we are booked to stay in a *rifugio*. *Rifugi* are found all over the Italian mountains. Often completely isolated, they are havens providing shelter, often food and sometimes a bed. Ours offers accommodation in one of the restored stone buildings and has a very good restaurant. We settle into our room and then climb the last leg of the mountain by foot to get to the castle remains and a lone, spectacular church sitting as close to God as a person can get. The 360-degree views of the national park are breathtaking.

The warm gusty wind reminds us how high we are and as we walk through the ruins we marvel at the tenacity of the people who built in such an unforgiving environment. I can only imagine how forbidding the castle would be in the depths of winter. From here I can see my Maiella Mountain below, as well as all the other spectacular mountains and plains. Further down are the green valleys where the saffron and lentils are grown. As we sit admiring the view the wind carries with it the gentle sound of bells, another reminder of the shepherds and their sheep grazing below.

The next day we say goodbye to the *Campo Imperatore* and head through endless almond groves to the coldest capital city in Italy, L'Aquila. It is a very old city with a huge fortressed castle built by its once Spanish rulers in the sixteenth century. The city of L'Aquila was formed by the citizens of the surrounding ninety-nine villages so the number ninety-nine plays an important role in this town. There are ninety-nine piazzas, churches and fountains, although not all have survived the passage of time, wars and natural disasters. But the *fontana delle novantanove cannelle* (fountain with ninety-nine spouts) still spouts water as a testament to those founding villages. However, the huge fountain's three walls have only ninety-three different faces squirting water from their mouths. I find another six small spouts at one end, making up the ninety-nine, perhaps the result of an oversight or perhaps because some villages did not pay their share.

We stop at L'Aquila's famous *Fratelli Nurzia* pastry shop for their particular take on coffee. Here it is served with warm milk and a slab of chocolate *torrone* (nougat) bobbing in the cup. As you stir, the chocolate melts and the nutty chocolate flavour infuses the coffee. It is so good I buy a five-pack of *torrone* to take home.

Despite our caffeine boost it is over 35 degrees Celsius and walking all over L'Aquila visiting churches, piazzas, fountains and streets takes its toll. We jump into the air-conditioned car and head for home past the almond groves, saffron fields and rocky mountains, back to the patchwork farmland and green Maiella of home.

At the height of summer my brother Simon spends a week with me at Capoposta. We fit in a little touring amidst a very busy schedule based around visiting family, eating, drinking countless cups of coffee and paying our respects to everyone in the neighbourhood. It is exhausting but lovely. He has brought with him a DVD of our family. Dad has recorded a message to everyone in stuttering Italian that is heartbreaking to watch but I think now they understand what his disease is doing to him. His speech becomes significantly clearer when he speaks directly to me, '*Angela—Torna qui!*' 'Angela, come home!'

The DVD ends with Dad playing his accordion. The joy in people's faces as they watch him is just beautiful. Grown men weep and stories always follow of Dad playing to enthusiastic party-goers back in the early 1950s. At one stage I am struck by the scene before me. Simon is sitting in the front yard of my cousin Nicola's house with the mountain in the background, on his lap his computer is open with the DVD of Dad playing. Sitting next to him watching attentively are five-year-old Mario, Zia Giulia, who is well into her eighties, and old Palmerino, who always recounts to me the date and almost the time Dad left for Australia. Dad last played accordion in Italy at Zia Giulia's wedding not long before he came to Australia. Yet here are three generations, sitting together watching him play.

When people here recall Dad they remember his music. He is 'Valentino with *Bianchoni*', his white accordion. At a *festa* I hear a local accordion player play a beautiful and intricate traditional tune. I mention to my uncle how beautiful it is. He looks at me and says, 'Valentino played this song.' I am dumbfounded. It is so intricate and rhythmic; I can't believe that my dad was ever so good. When he came to Australia, Dad stopped playing accordion for a long time.

What would make a man stop playing an instrument that was such an important part of his life, his identity? Was it too Italian? Was he too busy? Or did it just make him too homesick?

It was Dad's Alzheimer's that inspired us to buy him an accordion, something to get his brain working and keep him occupied. But it is his Alzheimer's that prevents me hearing him play the beautiful song I hear at the *festa*. It saddens me that I have lived a life without Dad and his music, and it saddens me more that he has lived his life in Australia this way. It seems such a sacrifice, a sacrifice I will never understand.

Having Simon with me, I am reminded of how hard it is to be surrounded by people you don't understand. Simon has a constantly dazed look that I easily recognise, exacerbated by the pressure of being our father's representative. Everything we say and do is a reflection on him. For our relatives, they can best show their hospitality through food, a way of communicating that doesn't require words, a natural point of commonality. For me it is just nice to have someone here who knows and understands everything I feel about Capoposta, the people, the stress, the emotion and the joy.

Hot nights, cool ice
and the sea

I'M IN SICILY. The food is unbelievable, the people vivacious, and the whole place is a bit wild, very spirited, very traditional, very colourful and very poor. I'm spending a month in beautiful Syracuse and attending language school every day.

A piazza of fragile yellow-white stone structures arcs around the *duomo* of Ortigia. All the buildings here are made of this brittle limestone, set with ornate metal balconies. As the stone ages it develops black speckles. The city is a maze of narrow streets overcrowded with life, balconies, palm trees and washing. I'm staying on one of these little lanes, too slender for a car. In the old quarter of Ortigia, tucked behind portal number 10 in Via San Paulo, are three apartments, one of which is mine. I walk through the dark courtyard and climb the narrow steps to my front door. It is student accommodation and pretty basic, with dodgy wiring and a rickety front door. But it is comfortable and has air-conditioning, a godsend as Syracuse is like a cauldron. The neighbours say hello through the kitchen window and I can hear the goings on of everyone around me. This is my home for the next four weeks.

Ortigia, actually a small island next to Syracuse, is a maze of old buildings, *piazze* and *palazzi*, surrounded by fishing boats, promenades and forts. It is a magical place that shines in the summer sunshine. There is something syrupy about the light as it glows off the blue sea and glides up over the old stone buildings. It's at its most luscious in the early evening when the heat of the day subsides and the sun, a glowing orb of fire, gently slips below the horizon. As the water glistens, giant flocks of swallows swoop in gentle cloud-like shapes, settling into large trees by the water and chirping so loudly it's like an invasion.

Nearly every day I sit on the steps of the *duomo*, relishing the shade, the soft breeze gently blowing up from the sea and the feel of my bare feet resting on the cool stone. It's my favourite spot in all Syracuse. Here I can watch the world go by, read the paper or, as I am now in the land of Inspector Moltalbano (my dream Italian man) read another instalment of these wonderful stories.

I often return to the *duomo* in the evenings. Nighttime in Sicily is when life happens. The streets are teeming with families, couples, young people and tourists doing the *passeggiata*. Here, as this is the really deep south, the *passeggiata* isn't just a walk but the centre of social existence. People dress beautifully and wander the streets, escaping the humidity of their houses and enjoying the cool breeze of the night. Kids too are out until midnight. Sitting in the piazza I watch whole dramas unfold: family disputes, lovers meeting, long-lost friends catching up, old ladies gossiping, old men giving advice to anyone who goes past, and kids playing football. There's a hum in the air and the noise drifts up and around the buildings.

Just near my apartment, the Ortigia fresh food market is an explosion of colour, smells and sounds. Stallholders call out constantly, enticing you to buy their produce. The market is bursting with everything that is southern—tomatoes, dried tomatoes, tomato paste, olives, bunches of dried oregano, huge buckets of capers, eggplants the size of melons, bright capsicums, zucchinis of every shape and size, and ever-present are huge slabs of swordfish, Syracuse's favourite. It is cooked in many different ways here, in tomato sauce with pasta, roasted, grilled with lemon, or rolled with pine nuts and sultanas.

It is not the fish that entrances me though, but the roasted vegetable stands. At one stand located under a series of old, faded and torn umbrellas stands a weatherworn lady well into her seventies. She has a huge open barbecue filled with hot coals in which she roasts not just capsicums, but whole onions, eggplants and tomatoes. Her produce is displayed in old pots—all charred, black and smoky—and she weighs orders on scales from another century. As I stand watching her, sipping on granita to allay the heat, it is like stepping back in time.

Granita is the perfect reprieve for the soaring temperatures. Ice and fruit juice, particularly lemon, is crushed into a smooth, icy, silky pulp and eaten with a spoon from a glass. It is a refreshing sweet dish after an *arancini*, a large pear-shaped rice ball coated in breadcrumbs and filled with a variety of delights—my favourite is *ragu* with hard-boiled egg, chunks of mozzarella and peas. These crispy on the outside, gooey in the middle delights make the ideal lunch.

Pasta is served slightly differently here. Instead of the usual parmesan cheese scattered on top, often Sicilian pasta dishes, especially vegetarian ones originating from the mountain areas, have crushed pistachio, crushed almonds or fried breadcrumbs, *mollica*, sprinkled over them. One in particular, a combination of pumpkin, mint, almonds, cheese and pistachio, truly captures the Greek, Arab, African and Mediterranean influences present in Sicily.

Pasta with pistachio nuts

spaghetti
1 garlic clove, finely sliced
olive oil
pistachio nuts, crushed
mint, finely chopped
pecorino cheese
cracked pepper

Cook spaghetti in well-salted water. Meanwhile, place the garlic in a large pan with a good amount of oil. Just as the pasta is about ready, turn the heat on for the pan. Add the pasta to the pan with some of the pasta water. Sprinkle with crushed pistachio nuts, mint and some *pecorino* cheese. Toss well. Serve with cracked pepper and sprinkle with more *pecorino* cheese.

I have also become addicted to fennel and orange salad. While this is a salad I've often made in Australia, it originates from Sicily and takes on another dimension here. I prepare it for myself every day for a week. A symbol of Sicilian decadence and another favourite is gelato stuffed in a brioche. It is very common early in the morning to see old men in the piazza munching on these treats, often filled with pistachio ice-cream. Then there's all the standard Sicilian fare that just seems to taste a thousand times better when eaten in Sicily. A real *pasta alla norma* is something to behold. *Norma* is pasta with tomatoes and eggplant. It has grated smoked, baked, or salted ricotta sprinkled on top. It's a bit pungent and full bodied and goes perfectly with the eggplant. Along with the cannoli, swordfish, pistachio biscuits, marzipan sweets—I am in paradise.

Sicilian fennel salad

The chilli and onion are essential to this dish, giving it bite, punch and personality.

> 1 fennel bulb, finely sliced
> dried oregano
> dried chilli flakes
> ¼ red onion, finely sliced
> salt and pepper
> 1 orange
> olive oil

Wash the fennel well and place in a salad bowl with a sprinkling of oregano, chilli flakes, the red onion, salt and pepper. To this, add an orange that has been segmented so that there is no pith or membrane. Drizzle the salad with olive oil and toss well.

I escape the heat whenever I can by retreating to a local beach. The seaside that surrounds Ortigia is rocky but

I manage to find a tiny patch of sand next to a marina filled with colourful fishing boats. I go early in the morning but already all around me are several *pensioni* with their incredibly dark tans, brief bikinis, full pot bellies and constant talking, along with a few kids and their families. The water is still. I approach one of the old men, '*Scusa, è pulito?*' 'Is it clean?' He looks confused and then proceeds to tell me that as I can see, he and his friends are here and swim every day and he's happy to have his grandchildren swim here, so yes, it's clean.

Firmly back in my place, I find a spot on the sand and settle in. The water is indeed beautiful and the perfect temperature. I go most days to this tiny beach, and sure enough the old man and his grandchildren and gossiping friends are there every day, morning and afternoon, only going home for lunch and siesta. I love eavesdropping on their conversations about politics, neighbours, grandchildren who don't visit enough, the cost of living and the weather. I am jealous of this life spent at the beach each day in the company of friends.

On my second weekend in Sicily I go to Taormina and Noto. Taormina is a popular touristy area north of Syracuse with prices to match, but it's immediately apparent why it's been the holiday resort of choice for VIPs for over a century. The train station alone is a delight, with its beautiful, ornate, frescoed wooden ceiling, intricately carved furniture and view across the ocean. Taormina itself sits high above the sea. As the bus winds its way up to the centre of town we pass colourful villas with spectacular gardens. Through an impressive arch marked with a large palm tree the main street meanders, stopping every so often at the piazzas built into the edge of the hill. High in Taormina sits a dark red stone Greek amphitheatre with a view hazy with humidity, dotted with tall trees and palms and stretching to the coast, while in the distance Mount Etna looms. I imagine the splendour of viewing Greek tragedies at sunset in ancient times and wonder at how these structures still stand, having borne witness to thousands of years of humanity.

South of Syracuse and a short bus ride away is Noto, an important noble town that was destroyed in the 1600s by an earthquake. It has been completely rebuilt in the baroque style and is one of the most wondrous examples of this grotesque and elaborate architecture. The *duomo* in Noto is particularly spectacular, rising up from the main street with grand steps. As I enter I encounter a choir preparing for a special mass. I ask one of the ladies in the congregation what the mass is for and she points above the altar to a heavy silver urn, explaining that it holds the remnants of the patron saint of Noto, San Corrado. Twice a year the giant urn is carried through the city streets of Noto, a parade held to celebrate his sainthood. I stay and goosebumps prickle my arms as the choir's singing resonates high into the dome and throughout the cathedral. I fit perfectly into this congregation;

I am short, dark-haired, rotund and waving a fan in front of my face to keep from fainting in the heat. An authentic Sicilian.

From Syracuse, I make the long bus trip through the centre of Sicily for a weekend in Palermo. The landscape of central Sicily is very different from that of the coast. It is stark and treeless with endless rolling hills of yellow and brown. The earth seems dry, as though it has never rained here. The houses appear run-down and are few and far between.

Palermo itself is hot, seething, dirty and poor. But I have made the trek to Palermo especially to see the mosaics and I am not disappointed. As I walk into the *Cappella Palatina* it literally takes my breath away. I am almost brought to tears and as I catch my breath I look at the security guard who is smiling at me. He ushers me in with pride. All around me are tiny pieces of marble, stone and ceramic finely covered in gold and luminously depicting biblical tales.

Despite the beauty of the mosaics I am glad not to be spending too long in Palermo. The city is truly chaotic, overcrowded buses pause for but a second and I'm in constant fear of missing my stop. The traffic is insane, pedestrian crossings are a nightmare and I feel quite unsafe walking Palermo's narrow paths and dark lanes.

I do, however, explore some of the smaller streets that make up the old quarters of Palermo. These neighbourhoods are boisterous, energetic and crowded with life. As with most of Italy people shout from their balconies or to each other as they walk along the street, calling out to children or friends, and as always everywhere there are kids playing soccer. But the streets here are dirty and the shops basic and poor.

Palermo is sweltering, humid, sticky and intense. I sweat continuously and as it runs down my back and drips down my legs the heat overwhelms me. I feel faint and find myself vomiting in the street of a dubious neighbourhood. I am physically and mentally exhausted. Perhaps after such a long time travelling on my own I am tiring of the stress and responsibility of it.

I have been thinking about home a lot lately. My conversations are only with Mum now. Dad doesn't feel comfortable talking on the phone anymore, not even with his daughter. When I call, Mum tells him it's me. He asks where I am and Mum replies, 'Italy.' His next question is always the same: 'When is she coming home?' Soon, Dad ... soon.

Autumn

Wedding bells, gladiators and gnome houses

I DRAG MYSELF away from the gelati and cannoli of Sicily and head for Rome where I meet up with my friends from home, Gavin and Janine. Their visit is perfectly timed. We are to spend two weeks together and I can't wait for the endless chatter and banter in English and with Australians.

Every time I am in Rome I'm struck by the sheer scale of the city and the fact that modern life happens amid buildings, streets and neighbourhoods that have hummed with life for thousands of years. Ruins are scattered everywhere, yet somehow Romans have a way of continuing their mad, crazy and chaotic existence amongst the monuments.

We walk nearly every pavement in the city before spending a day at the Colosseum, Palatine Hill and

Roman Forum. Despite previous visits to Rome I have saved these sights until now so it is equally exciting for us all. You can almost hear the roar of the crowd, the lions and the cries of pain from the thousands of people and animals who were slaughtered in this brutal place.

We have many memorable moments together in Rome, some better than others. The buses are frequent and cheap here and we use them regularly to weave our way from sight to sight. On one such trip we are crammed in tightly, almost unable to move. A gypsy woman with an infant child works her way through the crowded bus and stands directly in front of Gavin. She is breastfeeding her baby and this proves an effective distraction as she pushes up against him. He reaches for the strap overhead to keep his balance as the bus moves, and underneath the cover of the child's swathe the woman deftly gets her fingers into his bum bag and removes what euros he has in there. It happens before my eyes and I call out but by the time Gavin realises what is going on, she is off the bus. I think about that child for many days after this incident, and the future already laid out for it.

It feels good to show off some of my Italian know-how and language skills with Gavin and Janine. I give them some cultural tips, including a warning not to order a coffee with milk after 11 am. They manage to restrain themselves for much of the trip, when after lunch Gavin innocently asks for a *café macchiato*, literally coffee with just a tiny drop of milk. The waiter pauses, looks at him for a moment then says, '*No. Assolutamente no! Devi bere un espresso!*' 'No way! You have to drink an espresso!'

For the next leg of our adventure we hire a car. We drive from Termini Station right through the centre of Rome and on to Abruzzo. We're heading home for a few days so I can attend my cousin Peppino's wedding. Somehow we manage to find our way out of the city with the help of Gavin's compass and scouting skills and my newly acquired driving expertise. Gavin and Janine are looking forward to seeing the Abruzzo I've talked about constantly since their arrival.

We settle into Maria Chiara's apartment in Casoli, our base for the next few days. I show them proudly around the farm, countryside, villages and mountain that has become my own. Zia and Zio proudly play host for a couple of meals together. Zia Rosaria outdoes herself, cooking delectable dishes for the foreign visitors. Watching Gavin lick his fingers with satisfaction after sampling her roasted rabbit is a joy.

Zia Rosaria's melting coniglio
Rabbit

> rabbit pieces soaked in water and vinegar
> garlic
> mixed fresh herbs
> salt
> ground coriander

olive oil
vegetables

Marinate small pieces of good farmed rabbit in lots of garlic, herbs, salt and ground coriander. Brown in a pan with olive oil. Add water to halfway up the height of the meat and gently simmer covered for about 1½ hours. You may need to add more water as it cooks. At this stage of the cooking it doesn't look very nice, with the meat looking like it is stewing in water, but be patient.

After a period of simmering, add vegetables. You can add carrot pieces and peas, or some potatoes, or onion and capsicums, depending on your tastes and what's in the larder. Keep cooking. Eventually the water will evaporate completely and the meat will brown nicely. All you will have left is sticky, melt-in-your-mouth meat and vegies flavoured and caramelised with the meat juices. My family fights to get the joy of scraping the cooking pan with bread to get every last bit of stickiness.

This rabbit is truly delicious. You must use good farmed rabbit that has been soaked in water with vinegar. You can use this method for chicken as well, but don't cook chicken as long as rabbit.

This can also be cooked under a *coppo* on a wood fire floor or a camp oven covered with coals.

I leave Gavin and Janine to explore Chieti province for a day while I attend Peppino's wedding. Peppino lives next door to Zio Alberto in Capoposta. He has the Di Sciascio eyes that sparkle blue.

Italians love a wedding. Ever since I arrived they have been working on the house, renovating it in readiness for the new couple. In Abruzzo, the family home is often converted to a two-family home when a son marries. Their farmhouse now has a new apartment on the second floor. It's a huge investment and adds to the growing anticipation that builds as the day of the wedding approaches.

Two weeks before, as is Casolani tradition, the house is opened to all guests that are invited to the wedding. Usually, this is when wedding presents are given, along with a house-warming gift. It's a big party and an opportunity for the couple to show off their new home. Traditionally this is also when the bride displays her trousseau, all the beautiful manchester she has spent her teenage years making, weaving the linen and then embroidering it. Today many of the craft traditions are slowly being lost as the generations pass and most pieces are bought from shops.

One week before the wedding *la cena* is held, basically another wedding reception for B-list guests. It is just as big as the wedding but without the ceremony or the dress.

Finally the day of the actual wedding arrives. As guests of the groom we go to his house an hour before the ceremony. Here we are offered champagne, coffee, beer and other drinks, as well as sweet and savoury breakfast treats, along with some *confetti* (not paper confetti, but the famous sugar-coated almonds from Sulmona in Abruzzo), a small bag of coloured rice, and a ribbon to tie to our cars. While we are all wishing the groom and his family well a similar ceremony is happening at the bride's house with her guests.

Next we all pile into our cars and the convoy heads for the church, horns tooting all the way. All the villagers are out to watch the spectacle and wish the couple luck. Meanwhile, back at the house, as is tradition, two of my cousins are looking after the home and farm for the family. They have already served us breakfast and now they will clean up, milk the cows and tend the animals until everyone returns late that night.

We wait eagerly at the church for the bride and all her guests to arrive. From within we can hear more car horns so we know they must be close by. My cousin stiffens as he realises how close he is to the biggest commitment of his life. His father, Biasetto, who is admittedly an emotional man, does not stop crying all day. When I greeted him this morning he burst into tears. Later when we left the house, he burst into tears. During the ceremony, he will burst into tears and all through the reception and as we dance together, he will burst into tears. I remember watching him as he viewed the DVD of Valentino playing his accordion; he wept like a baby. His emotions are contagious. I am crying now just thinking about it. Italian men are not afraid to show how they feel. My uncles and cousins are all emotional too, as is my dear dad. My brothers Matt and Michael cry over the smallest thing and I can be reduced to tears by ads on television, much to the annoyance and horror of my brother Simon. Clearly the Capoposta crying gene has somehow skipped him.

The Catholic ceremony is long and in an Italian I struggle to understand. The church is filled with smartly dressed relatives, the groom's guests to the right, the bride's on the left. The church is old but well maintained and a large marble altar stands proudly before the congregation. The bride finally enters, walking up the aisle accompanied only by her father, whose arm is linked proudly through hers. There are no bridesmaids or flower girls in Italian weddings. Instead the bride and groom each select a witness and it is they who take on the role of what we would call the maid of honour and best man. However, in Italy they are allowed to wear whatever they like and the female witness doesn't have to hold the requisite bouquet of flowers.

Melissa, the bride, teaches Sunday school and her students stand proudly on the altar. They sing in chorus during the ceremony and read touching prayers to the couple. Unlike weddings in Australia, the bride and the groom are the last to leave the church. We stand out the front holding ribbons that criss-cross the path from the door, and as we throw our rice at the couple they throw *confetti* back to us while the groom cuts their way through the ribbons. They smile broadly with happiness and I presume a sense of relief. Melissa is glowing in a dress of flowing cream lace and Peppino holds her hand proudly. Then champagne corks are popping and everyone is hip-hip-hooraying. Soon we all pile back into our cars and the convoy honks its way to the reception.

We arrive to an incredible party. Food plays a very important role in any festive occasion in Italy and weddings are the perfect opportunity for the couple's families to show off their prosperity, style and hospitality. We work our way through many courses: a seafood buffet to start, then seafood *agnolotti* pasta, then seafood *chitarra* pasta, then a roast fillet of fish, then sorbet, then roast veal, then wedding cake, and finally a fruit and dessert buffet. Thankfully there is also lots and lots of dancing. The band plays an irresistible mixture of traditional and modern songs but the traditional ones prove the most popular. Italians love to dance and almost everyone is up enjoying the music for much of the evening. It is such fun to simply dance the night away uninterrupted by the speeches, telegrams, bridal waltzes and the like that usually interrupt proceedings back home.

The dancing is, however, halted momentarily for some rather entertaining informal traditions. The couple's friends have prepared a series of games in advance for the newlyweds to endure and it's our job to cheer them on. In one, Peppino has to pop several balloons that have been belted around Melissa's waist. To do this, he is expected to use a banana covered in pins hanging between his legs. He is reasonably successful, if rather red-faced by the end of it.

Later in the evening the dancing again stops and we gather around a large video screen. Peppino and Melissa made a video prior to the wedding—a sort of testament to their love. We cheer and heckle, especially when the couple kisses on screen. I find it all quite entrancing, as does one of Peppino's cousins from Canada. We stand close, sharing our amazement and fascination with the peculiar customs being played out before us.

Finally, late in the evening, and after several nips of *nocino*, we bid farewell to the couple and, *bomboniere* gift in hand, I crawl home to bed.

Nocino

This is a traditional digestive liqueur of our area. Many families make this and if you manage to get through a full Abruzzesse lunch, a nip of *nocino* does wonders for your stomach. After a wedding feast, your stomach certainly needs it!

> 13 fresh walnuts (they need to be tender—able to
>   be sliced shell and all)
> 400 g 95% alcohol
> 60 g sugar
> 1 stick cinnamon

grated nutmeg
4 cloves

Cut the walnuts in half but don't use metal as this
will increase oxidisation. Put the walnuts in a jar
with the alcohol. Close the lid and leave the jar in
a warm sunny place for twenty days. Then add the
spices and sugar and leave sealed for another twenty
days. Filter and bottle.

My wedding obligations completed, Gavin, Janine and
I set off rather early for a four-hour drive south to
Alberobello in Puglia. While I sleep off my late night
Gavin braves the madness of an Italian motorway.
Alberobello is *Trulli* house territory. *Trulli* houses are
small circular homes painted white with a grey stone
conical roof. Occasionally these roofs have large pagan
symbols painted on them but the houses themselves
are reminiscent of the gnome homes of my childhood
fairytales.

We arrive in Alberobello for lunch and are won-
derstruck by the quaintness of the place. There are
Trulli houses everywhere and we are childishly excited
as we check into one of our very own for the night,
right in the centre of town. Again, the contrasts of Italy
astound me. Everything is painted white and it feels as
though we are in Greece.

Along with being the home of my favourite
bread, Pulgia is renowned for its preserved vegetable

antipasta and for producing lots and lots of olives. The dry Puglian countryside is covered with olive trees. The famous pastas of Puglia are *orecchiette*, *cavatelli* and *fricelli*, all made without eggs, and the most well known Pugliese pasta sauce is *cime di rapa*, made from turnip tops.

Orriechiette con cime di rapa
Orriechietti with turnip tops

Rapa (turnip tops) is a popular vegetable in the south of Italy and is sometimes known as *broccoletti*. If turnip tops are hard to find, I have substituted Chinese broccoli, or even *broccolini*, and this works well.

> *rapa* (turnip tops)
> 1 garlic clove, finely chopped
> 3 or 4 anchovies, chopped
> olive oil
> dried chilli flakes (optional)
> *orriechiette* pasta

Chop and par cook the *rapa* in the pasta water. Remove the *rapa* and add to a large pan with the garlic, anchovies, a serious swig of olive oil and a little of the pasta water. If you like, add some dried chilli flakes. Cook the *orriechiette*, then add it to the pan and heat, tossing until the anchovies have melted. Serve without cheese.

Alternatively, slowly heat the oil with a smashed garlic clove and the anchovies. Avoid frying the anchovies as they turn bitter; instead, gently heat them so that they melt into the oil. The best way to do this is to hold a pan over the boiling pasta water rather than the flame of a stove. Remove the garlic clove before serving.

Don't be scared of anchovies. Used in this way they lose their consistency and add a delicate, deep yet subtle salty flavour to the dish. Try the same recipe with cauliflower ... it's delicious.

The Puglian coast is sandy, stark and relatively resort-free, yet the water in Puglia is crystal clear and the coastline exquisite. As we drive we are dwarfed by the hundreds of ancient and wizened olive trees we pass, some with trunks as wide as a Fiat 500. While exploring, we literally stumble across a huge Roman archaeological site that isn't on our maps or in our guide books. We watch students surveying the remains of a temple, houses and an amphitheatre before heading for Matera.

Matera is in Basilicata. Only an hour from the rolling hills, rich red earth, rocky terrain and rustic stone walls of Alberobello, we find ourselves entering a land of dry, brown, treeless fields with very few houses and I am reminded of the starkness of central Sicily.

We have come here to see the cave dwellings, the *sassi* of Matera.

Up until the 1950s entire families, along with all their animals (horses, maybe a cow, chickens and so on), lived together in houses created from caves dug into the walls of a large ravine. Living conditions were abominable with an infant mortality rate of fifty percent. Thankfully the poverty and despair has gone now. Indeed the town now houses a music conservatory and we wonder at the contrast as we listen to the beautiful sound of piano and flute drifting out of the windows and bouncing off the walls of the narrow streets. It is a remarkable place, with churches, houses, shops, everything built into the grottos of the ravine. Matera remains an eerie place, however, perhaps because of all the suffering that has come before, and we are glad to return to the carefree charms of Alberobello.

Back in Capoposta, I bid farewell to my dear friends. We managed to pack a lot into two short weeks together and I am sad to see them go. As they prepare to depart they remark on the beauty of the olive trees. They are now rich with fruit that shines in the autumn sun and the trees glow like expectant mothers. Since arriving I have delighted in watching the seasons change through the olive trees and in November they'll be ready for harvest. It's incredibly hard, back-breaking work and needs all the hands that can be mustered. I will plan my remaining two months of travel around the harvest.

The seasons change quite quickly here, literally in a day. The rains have begun and snow is appearing on the top of the Maiella Mountain. My summer wardrobe went home with Gavin and Janine and tonight I wear boots and tights for the first time in months. The beach goers have left, the umbrellas packed away for another year, and the seaside is deserted again. I see rich golden hues all around me as I traverse the area. The vines are groaning under the weight of heavy, healthy bunches of sweet fruit and the mountain trees have all the colours of autumn, rust reds, golds and browns. The autumn sky shines blue and a magical light, golden and timid, seduces me into watching the shadows bouncing off the rocky mountain walls. It's a different light, moody and rich and velvety and teasingly warm on my back. But as soon as it hides away, the crisp cool air reminds me that summer is over.

This week is the *Festa di Santa Reparata*, the annual *festa* of Casoli. The streets are bejewelled with ornate lights and there are bands, food stalls, dancing in the streets, concerts and parades. The *festa* celebrates the patron saint of Casoli and lasts for three days, but the middle day is the most important. This is the day of the huge street parade when all the children have the day off school. It is quite simply fantastic. As I step into the street everyone is resplendent and proud, dressed in their finest. Old couples have left their fields and farms for the day and teenagers, adults and children all mingle, catching up with friends. There is a wonderful sense of culture, tradition and pride. A pride I share.

As the parade begins, adults and children head towards the church carrying gifts to be blessed. Many are in traditional dress and the women carry large copper pots filled with cakes and other treats on their heads. These pots were once used to carry water to and from the wells, and my mum remembers seeing them used in this way when she first came to Italy in 1974. There are also people wearing *chiochie*, traditional handcrafted shoes made of pigskin, and I recall Peppino's grandmother wearing these as her regular footwear in 1993 on my first trip to Capoposta.

Next follows a series of tractors pulling floats decorated and stocked with food and treats, each from a different village in the Casoli area. Capoposta has joined with three other small villages and its tractor looks magnificent, stocked with homemade breads, cakes, cheeses and salamis all donated by the residents. On one float people are stomping on grapes; on another carrying an old flour mill, women are making pasta. Many display *porchetta* or large *provolone* cheeses. They all make their way to the church where the priest blesses everything and everyone. Then they park in the street and we all flock around buying the food that's been donated, with the proceeds going to the *festa* and the church. Last year they raised over 20 000 euros.

In the evening I head back to town. There is to be a concert and the streets have been transformed into an enchanted fairy kingdom with pretty lights sparkling from huge, ornate wooden frames arching across the street at thirty-metre intervals. The night ends with chest-thumping fireworks.

Fireworks are taken very seriously in Italy. Every village ends their *festa* with fireworks and there is great rivalry to create the wildest display. All through the summer months the bangs and hisses of fireworks have been heard up and down the valley. The Fossacesia *festa* stages an awesome display over the sea with thousands of people flocking to the seaside town to sit on the beach and watch in wonder as the night sky explodes with a brilliant pyrotechnic display. That same crowd then returns to their cars and the tradition of the great Italian traffic jam commences once more as everyone inches and honks their way home.

Home feels very close now. My bank account is nearly empty, my week in New York in December seeming more and more expensive each day as what remains of my life savings slides into oblivion with the stock market crisis. But right now, here, none of this seems to matter.

Chestnuts, golden light and polenta

IN ITALY ALL of daily life reflects and respects the seasons. It is autumn now so Italians are wearing their autumn wardrobe, their spring and summer clothes having been packed away. Perhaps it is all part of the aesthetic. Italians desire harmony and as such believe that how you present yourself needs to be part of a larger symphony, with each individual and their surroundings all playing a part. Italian food is no different: pumpkin (although not in Abruzzo), chestnuts, apples and grapes in autumn; fennel and oranges in winter; asparagus in the spring; and eggplant, zucchini and tomatoes in summer. Eating this way makes me feel more connected to the earth and brings with it a sense of order and anticipation. All is in tune, the symphony is at work.

I contrast this with Australia where broccoli can be bought all year round, few people seem to know what vegetable is in season when and the focus appears to be on quantity, not quality. Rather than dressing to conform we take pride in our individuality and shun those who dare to judge us on our personal presentation. Being here has taught me to appreciate that regardless of who we are we shouldn't compromise on quality; that it is at times better to have less than more. I only hope I can carry this wisdom with me when I return.

In early October, after the Casoli festival, I head off on my farewell tour of Italy. I spend a couple of weeks in Lombardy and then Le Marche. In Bergamo I walk through a chestnut forest with my cousin Anna; we share a blissful autumn experience. The chestnut trees stand spaced out, tall and clear, so that every leaf gets its fair share of the sun. The colours are a magical mix of brown, yellow, gold and green, creating a rainbow of autumn shades contrasting magnificently with the clear blue sky. We walk for nearly two hours, our feet crunching their way through the floor of leaves. The only sounds we hear are the birds, rustling branches and the occasional gentle thud as a chestnut pod releases its hold and softly lands on the cushion of leaves below, with just enough force to open its spiky pod and expose the three or four richly coloured chestnuts snuggled inside. Anna calls this '*un bombardamento di castagna*', 'a bombardment of chestnuts'. Our tranquillity is momentarily disturbed only by the echo of gunshots. With autumn comes bird-hunting season in Bergamo.

While in Bergamo, our good family friends Adriano and Giuliana visit from Como and we share a meal together of *pasta chitarra*, *arrosto morto* and a most delightful cake made by Giuliana. She foraged for the chestnuts the day before, boiling them up until their centres were white, and then had her husband undertake the painstaking task of scooping out the centres and mashing them through a sieve, twice. The chestnut mixture was then re-boiled, left to cool, added to a sugar and egg mix and then folded through beaten egg whites. Served with cream, the cake is light, fluffy, and has a gentle flavour. It is like having the chestnut forest on a plate.

Arrosto morto
Dead roast

Use a good piece of roast meat such as *girello* veal, boned rolled lamb leg, a rolled turkey leg, boned and rolled rabbit or other such meat. If it is rolled meat, you can add garlic and herbs to the stuffing, even carrot, cheese (with a high melting point) and onion. I've even had it with an egg frittata included in the meat stuffing when rolled.

roasting meat
pancetta
rosemary or preferred herbs
salt
shallots
broth
potatoes (if needed)

Top the meat with pancetta and rosemary (or the appropriate herb for the meat) and season with salt (not too much). Tie with kitchen string and brown in a casserole dish or heavy-based pan. Remove the meat. Add some chopped shallots to the pan and soften.

Return the meat to the pan and add hot broth, enough to come halfway up the side of the meat. Be careful with the salt content of the broth.

Loosely cover and simmer gently for 2–3 hours. The long cooking time will intensify the salt flavour, which is why you should be careful with salt content of the stock. If you use a commercial broth, I would not salt the meat. If you think the sauce is too salty, add a potato to soak up the salt, and then remove it at the end.

Cool overnight. Slice thinly when cool and conserve the sauce—it should be a wonderful jelly. Remove any fat from the top of the sauce.

Put slices of meat on a heat-resistant serving platter and top with the jelly. Cover with foil and gently reheat.

The meat will be tender and the sauce incredibly flavoursome. This is a great dish if you are having a dinner party or have to feed lots of people, as most of the work is done the day before.

In Lecco, a city snuggled between beautiful Lake Como and imposing, rocky mountains, I again stay with my friend Tiziana and her family. During this visit we take a steep funicular up to Piani d'Erna, where Tiziana's husband has a small and very old hunter's cottage. The view from the funicular over Lecco and the lake is as breathtaking as that of the rocky edge of the mountain we travel so close to. Once at the top we walk for about five minutes until we reach the cottage. It is completely surrounded by spectacular trees and the autumn leaves are as thick as a mattress on the ground.

We enter the cottage and set about lighting the fire and pot-belly stove, collecting water from the well and throwing open the windows to let in the autumn air. We play cards and eat huge Florentine steaks cooked over the fire and served with grilled polenta, all washed down with a good red.

As the days and nights grow cooler I find myself spending more and more evenings around a crackling fire, eating the more robust dishes of the north. In Lecco I eat polenta with rabbit, and in Fano, polenta with *stinco*, veal shin braised in beer. All over Italy, generations were raised on polenta and little else. While I adore the food of my region and the way my relatives cook, in reality the food they now eat every day was in the past enjoyed only sparingly. The meat they reared was sold, eggs were sold, olive oil was rare and precious and wheat flour saved for special occasions. Cured meat was reserved for guests only and wheat bread was saved for the old and visitors. My dad was raised on gritty cornmeal bread, weedy vegetables, polenta, and pasta made from flour and water. To this day, he can't even look at a plate of polenta; it reminds him too much of poverty and of times when things were so tough they couldn't eat pasta.

In Abruzzo my grandmother's polenta was served straight onto the wooden kitchen table and may have been topped with a tomato *sugo* and some cheese before being eaten with hands. Occasionally there may have been some pork or quail or *baccala* (salt-dried fish). In the north, polenta is eaten with braised meats. My friend Tiziana pours her polenta out onto a wet cloth and wraps it up into the shape of a round loaf of bread. She brings this to the table on a wooden board and then opens up the cloth to serve. She uses her grandmother's wooden polenta knife to cut and serve it. Juicy rabbit cooked slowly in white wine is then slopped on top.

Polenta is best cooked in a copper pot with a rounded bottom. Just before the water comes to the boil, it should be salted and the polenta gently sprinkled in and stirred. Then it's stir, stir, stir and stir for at least forty minutes until cooked. My cousin Giacinto adds some milk and butter near the end to lighten it. Adjust the proportion of water to polenta depending on how thick it needs to be. For instance, *baccala* is traditionally served with sloppy, 'wet' polenta.

Making polenta is backbreaking work. In our front room in Geelong, my parents have a picture of Dad's sisters cooking it over a fire in one of those huge copper pots. They are bent over, stirring the thick yellow glug with a huge wooden paddle. It is sweaty, hard work but they are smiling, perhaps because they know the photo will make its way back to their long lost brother. Indeed it's doubtful they would make polenta in this way anymore. Today there are special copper polenta pots with a motorised paddle attached that gently turns the polenta.

Polenta—Three ways

The following recipes use coarse polenta, not instant polenta. Polenta should take about 40 minutes to cook and requires constant stirring. Traditionally polenta was made in an unlined copper pot with a rounded bottom called a *paiolo*. Generally the ratios of liquid to polenta are four parts liquid to one part polenta. Water is used as the main liquid but you can substitute some of the liquid for milk, cream or stock, depending on what you want to serve the polenta with. If you want runny polenta (called wet polenta), add more liquid when cooking. Polenta should be served immediately while it is soft. If you want to slice and fry it, turn it out onto a wooden board and let it cool. It can then be sliced into any shape ready for grilling.

Madalena's stinco (veal shin) with polenta

veal shin
plain flour
olive oil
rosemary
bay leaf
sage
500 ml beer
polenta
water
milk
butter

Coat the veal in flour. Heat oil in a casserole dish or a heavy-based pan with a lid. Add rosemary, bay leaf and sage. Add meat, brown on all sides and season. Add the beer, cover and simmer on low heat for 2 hours. Remove any fat that settles on top of the sauce after cooling and allow the meat to cool completely so that it slices better. This can all be done the day before serving. To serve, slice and place the meat on a heat-resistant platter. Spoon the sauce over the meat (it should be like a jelly), gently reheat and serve with polenta.

Cook polenta at a ratio of 200 g of polenta to 1 lt of water. As the water is about to boil, add the polenta in a stream while stirring continuously. Keep stirring for at least 40 minutes. When nearly ready, add a small glass of milk and a couple of knobs of butter and stir through.

Tiziana's rabbit and polenta

rabbit pieces
oil
butter
rosemary
white wine
polenta

In a large pan with a lid, brown seasoned rabbit pieces in oil and butter with some rosemary. After it is well browned, add a glass of white wine and simmer at low heat with the lid on for an hour. Add water if you need to.

For the polenta, bring 8 cups of water to the boil. Just before the water comes to the boil, add 2 cups of polenta in a stream and stir. Stir continuously for 40 minutes until smooth. When finished, turn onto a damp cloth and wrap. Unwrap the cloth at the table and serve. The traditional method is to cut the polenta with a wooden knife. Serve rabbit and drizzle pan juices over the polenta.

Baccala con polenta
Salted cod fish with polenta—Abruzzese style

  baccala (salted cod fish)
  olive oil
  parsley
  onion, chopped
  garlic
  celery, chopped
  tomato pulp

Chop *baccala* into large pieces and soak in water for two days. Change water two or three times. *Baccala* can be frozen after this point.

Wash the *baccala* again and cut into serving portions. Put in a pan with oil, parsley, onion, garlic, celery and tomato pulp. Add some water. Do not add salt. Cook gently until the *sugo* is rich and the oil has split.

Serve over wet polenta.

I bid farewell to Lombardy, the lake and torrents of Lecco and the bells and birds of Bergamo. On the train ride south from Milan, I sit looking out the window and realise this is the last time this year I will see this view. I've done the Bologna to Milan train trip so many times while making my way around the north of Italy that I've become accustomed to the flat farming plains lying between these great cities. On this last trip, the vine leaves are red and golden and there is a fog over the fields, giving them a somewhat mournful air. Perhaps they are sad that I am leaving. The feeling is mutual.

In Capoposta all are busy sowing grain before start-ing in on harvesting the olive trees. It's a dicey game, deciding when to sow and when not to sow, based on the rain. The weather has been less predictable these last few years making it harder for farmers to rely on their built-up knowledge of the seasons. Instead everyone watches the nightly weather report as if it's news from God.

One evening we are disturbed by gale-force winds that keep everyone awake and continue blowing well into the next day. When the winds finally die down my aunt and uncle inspect the olive groves and are heartbroken to find some of the fruit has been blown off the trees. My aunt holds in her hand what were plump, nearly ripe olives before the storm. As they fall through her fingers to the earth below, tears pour down her cheeks. My uncle behaves as though he is in mourning. I suppose really he is.

Despite this setback, the harvest will go ahead as planned. My cousin Mattia and his uncle Zio Alberto work together on their lands like brothers. Mattia is the son of my father's eldest brother Camillo. They have inherited the land from Nonno Mattia. When olive picking season comes, both families help each other harvest. First is always Mattia's wife's olive grove in Cippolara. The plot is on a particularly steep gradient and is terrible back-breaking work to harvest. First, large, heavy nets are placed on the ground beneath the trees, and then mechanical olive pickers shake the olives from the trees. On the end of a long pole sit two mechanical hands with long fingers. These clap together, tickling the olives from the tree so that the olives rain down onto the nets below. While holding these contraptions vertical for eight hours a day is exhausting, it is better that the alternative—hand picking from ladders. The nets are then collected and kilos of olives are put into large plastic bins ready to go straight to the *frentoia* to be pressed. Olive trees are always planted on sloping ground so negotiating the terrain, laying, lifting and moving the large nets and dragging large sacks of olives is extremely hard work.

The village is completely silent during the olive harvest, with only those unable to work remaining at home. All over the valley the only sound filling the air is that of the generator-powered, hand-held olive pickers.

I return home after the first day sore and miserable, having been completely outgunned by my pensioner aunt and uncle. Zia Rosaria, who is bent over with osteoporosis, climbs trees like a teenager. It takes us three days to get the first lot of olives in and there is much smiling and joy once it is finished. Thankfully the rest of the groves are much flatter.

Despite, or perhaps because, the work is so hard the picnic lunch provided at olive harvest is astounding. Whoever owns the plot being harvested is responsible for the catering and this always includes fresh coffee, cakes, pasta, a main course meat dish, salad, fruit, *sambuca*, wine and sweets or chocolate. Today it is our turn and Maria Chiara and I spend the entire morning cooking. We take the lunch down to the grove all hot and steaming then spend the rest of the afternoon helping with the picking. Tomorrow will be the same, and the next day, and the next for another week or two until it is all over.

Mostaccioli

These biscuits are delicious and go wonderfully with coffee. The recipe makes a lot but they keep for a long time in a sealed biscuit tin. If the volume scares you, halve the recipe. They were very popular during the olive harvest when we needed something sweet in the afternoon to keep us going.

1 kg flour
15 g baking powder
450 g almonds, roasted and chopped
3 heaped tbsp cocoa
a good handful grated chocolate

5 eggs
75 ml oil
lemon or orange rind, grated
300 g honey
1 tbsp marsala

Mix all the dry ingredients together. Add the wet ingredients and mix well. Split into sections and form into flattened logs. Cut into little *biscotti* pieces about 1½–2 cm thick. Bake at 160°C in a fan-forced oven (180°C in a conventional oven) for 30 minutes or until ready.

We work a small plot of trees on the way to San Domenico. It is all done in a day. As we work I keep hearing '*Zio Valentino*'. I ask Mattia why everyone is talking about my dad and he tells me it's not actually Dad they're talking about, but that the biggest and oldest tree in the grove is named after him. Long ago it was a very tall tree and with the old hand system of using ladders and little cane baskets around their waists, olive harvesting was a labour no one enjoyed, including my dad. One time he made an excuse to go and collect the lunch from Zio Camillo's house to avoid picking that tree and from that day on it has been called Zio Valentino's tree.

Tomorrow we pick the grove my Nonno planted, the oldest grove of our family. I am looking forward to being amongst those trees. When my Nonno was younger he and his brothers had no land with olive trees. He worked for others and received ten kilos of olives a day in return; for every four baskets he filled, one was kept for his labour. He would take fresh broad beans for lunch—no bread, no pasta, just beans. He worked like this to earn enough olives to make oil for the family. As years went by he and his brothers slowly gathered enough money to buy land and plant their own olives. Today the trees of our extended family, which all came from those planted by Nonno and his brothers, will yield 20,000 kilograms of olives.

Fresh bread drizzled with thick, rich, green, velvety olive oil, freshly pressed the day before, fruity, peppery and aromatic. My tastebuds are in heaven. All the backbreaking work, the pruning, protecting and nurturing throughout the year culminating in a couple of weeks of relentless physical labour. All this to capture what lies hidden in this tiny fruit. Oil. Delicious and flavoursome. Fresh and abundant.

One of the essential dishes of Abruzzo is soup and after a big day of olive harvesting, there is nothing more refreshing, invigorating and sustaining. My aunt makes soup at least three times a week. The soup here is a clear broth and ranges from quite simple dishes based on water and pasta to elaborate recipes for feast days. They are both energising and comforting. My father likes to call this type of soup 'clean soup'. If he can see the bottom of the soup bowl, then it's a good soup. Often in Capoposta, after a full Abruzzese multi-course lunch, I relish the relief of a good *brodo* in the evening.

Brodo
Soup a variety of ways

Pastine—The quick soup
  salt
  olive oil
  parmesan rind
  risoni pasta
  1 egg
  parmesan cheese
  parsley

Boil water with some salt and oil and a piece of parmesan rind if you have it (keep them in your freezer after you've finished grating them). After the water has boiled and is flavoured, add *risoni* pasta and boil until cooked but still firm. Add an egg that has been beaten with some parmesan cheese. Stir with a fork to break up the egg. Add parsley and serve.

Minestra Abruzzese
  water
  salt
  olive oil
  1 small potato, chopped into small pieces
  1 carrot, finely chopped

celery, finely chopped
1 small onion
5 or 6 cherry tomatoes, squeezed open with
   your hands
risoni pasta

Boil water with some salt and oil and the vegetables.

If you have a piece of left-over meat from last night's dinner, chop it up and add at the initial boiling stage. This will add flavour.

Boil until the vegetables are cooked, then add *risoni*. Boil the pasta until cooked—it should still be firm. Serve with parmesan cheese.

If you have a good chicken broth, use that instead of plain water.

Festa brodo
Complete with stracciatelli and pizza rustica
This is a big, serious soup made with a stock that has been cooked for up to 6 hours. It is served on feast days or at special meals like Christmas. You need to make the *pizza rustica* beforehand.

Broth
   1 whole chicken
   celery
   onion
   carrot
   parsley
   olive oil

Make a large quantity of broth with a good-quality hen, celery, onion, carrot, parsley and a slurp of olive oil. Salt the broth at the end. Before serving, four things are added to the broth—*stracciatelli* mixture, *pallotine*, *pizza rustica* and *risoni* pasta.

Stracciatelli

cardoons

lemon

egg

parmesan

For this you will need cardoons, a variety of wild artichoke that resembles leafy celery. String and trim the cardoons and chop into small pieces. Boil in salted water with lemon until soft. This can take some time. Strain and cool. Mix with beaten egg and parmesan cheese. This is added to the hot soup to make the *stracciatelli*.

Pallotine

tiny meatballs, see *timballo* recipe (page 101)

eggs

cheese

Make tiny meatballs as for the *timballo* recipe. Mix with eggs and cheese and cook separately in a pot with some of the broth. Then add to the soup at serving.

Pizza rustica

1 egg

1 tbspn parmesan

1 tbspn plain flour
parsley, finely chopped

The proportions for this recipe are one egg to one spoon of parmesan cheese to one spoon of plain flour. Beat the egg white until stiff, then mix in the yolk, flour and cheese. Add parsley. Spread on a baking tray lined with paper. Spread 1–2 centimetres thick. Cook in the oven (it won't take long) then chop into small cubes. Zia Rosaria prepares this in large batches and then freezes it. (*Pizza rustica* is often referred to in recipe books as a pie filled with cheese and ham. In Capoposta, though, *pizza rustica* is only used to refer to these small pieces of pastry put in soup.)

Remove the meat and vegies from the broth. Add the pasta to the broth and cook. (If you are cooking a broth for a large number of people, it is better to cook the pasta in a separate pot with some of the broth, then add it to the plates.) Add the *stracciatelli* and *pallotine* to the soup so that the egg cooks. Put a small handful of *pizza rustica* into each soup bowl. Ladle the broth into each plate over the *pizza rustica*. Serve with parmesan.

A broth with home-grown *gallina* (hen) simmered for six hours is truly spectacular. At the table where I ate a version of this soup (*Carnevale*), there was absolute silence except for the slurping of the soup. You could sense the joy as people savoured this precious liquid.

In Teramo in north Abruzzo, they make a different version of this soup. Instead of pasta and *pizza rustica*, they make *scrippelle*. These are fine crepes; combine 110 g flour for every egg plus some water to make a wet mix, then cook like thin crepes. Each *scrippelle* is sprinkled with parmesan, rolled up and tied in a knot. A *scrippelle* is placed in every soup dish and the hot broth is poured over the top.

In Abruzzo, egg beaten with parmesan is used a lot in soups. In this recipe you can see that beaten egg is used with the *stracciatelli* and the *pallotine*. In Rome, they have a famous soup called only *stracciatelli*, which is plain chicken broth served with egg and cheese mixture, finely distributed throughout the soup. In Abruzzo the egg is chunky and stringy.

One evening my aunt makes a variation of this usually comforting soup that is somewhat confronting. After butchering a hen and a chicken that morning to sell to someone, she found inside the hen three eggs at various stages of development. Zia Rosaria removed these and kept them in water. Later that night, when we are having broth, instead of making the usual *stracciatelli* she pierces the lining of the yolks in the half-formed eggs and squeezes the thick yellow insides into the soup, where it forms long strings. She then pulls out a mass of egg-string and cuts it up before adding it to the soup again. I find the whole thing a little disturbing, I must confess, but the egg does add a real richness to the soup and I have to admit it has a heartier taste than normal egg yolk.

As my family in Australia turn their clocks forward my family in Italy turn theirs back. The nights suddenly get dark and cold even earlier, sending our own body clocks into a spin. We find ourselves craving dinner soon after lunch and everyone is going to bed earlier. Everyone but Zia Rosaria. The clock over the sink in her shed has remained on summer time for years. As far as she is concerned the world can do as it likes but she prefers summer time and lives her life by it, rising with the sun and milking the cows when they need it. For her, a clock has relevance only for timing the boiling of pasta and the keeping of appointments.

The news from home that my new niece Lucy has been born is still fresh when a neighbour runs to our back door rallying the men to help with a calving. I go over to their stable to be part of this minor miracle. Under the watchful eye of my uncle, the vet, three neighbours from the village and me, a little female calf enters the world. As it licks its skin and wobbles onto its feet I think of little Lucy wobbling her way through the first few weeks of her life. As with the animals in this stable, Lucy is in safe hands, family all around to hold her as she takes her first breaths, suckles her first meal, snuggles in her Nonno's arms for the first time and cries her first tears. At the thought of her in my own arms I smile.

I am woken one night by the sound of accordion music and singing coming from outside. I look out the window and there, gathered out the front of my neighbour's house, is a group of men, women and children, all singing loudly and calling out to my newlywed cousin Peppino and his wife. They sing and jeer until finally the couple emerges and invites them in for drinks and refreshments. It is all over in an hour and everyone goes back to their beds to sleep. Except me, who has absolutely no idea what I have just seen. Maria Chiara explains the next day that it is the custom for friends of a newlywed couple to often go to their house at midnight to sing and play music loudly to disturb their rest.

Thinking about the possible sleepless nights ahead I remember Dad telling me stories of him going to people's houses late at night to serenade a girl and, I presume, to play music with groups like this one. He says he always enjoyed playing for these events, even late at night, because he often got invited into the house and offered a good feed. Some mammas would even cook up a pasta to serve the accordion player.

There are a lot of cats in Capoposta. There are a lot of mice and a lot of rats and consequently, a lot of cats. Cats wait at our back door after lunch hoping for some leftover pasta to supplement what they can catch for themselves. Sometimes, my aunt cooks extra pasta because, '*i gatti sono magri*', the cats are skinny. It seems cats do eat pasta. In fact, all pets in Italy eat pasta. At the supermarket you can buy huge sacks of poor-quality pasta purely for feeding dogs. I see people put this pasta in the hot pasta water left from cooking the family's lunch and by the time lunch is over the dog pasta has softened and is ready to serve to the hungry animals waiting outside.

Other than her virtual delicatessen in the attic, Zia Rosaria has another favourite spot for storing food: under the stairwell near the back door. In this dark, cool place my aunt keeps the fruit and cured meat that we're currently eating. She prefers *il frigo naturale*, the natural fridge, for fruit and cured meats in use. One day, as I'm coming in from the backyard, a guilty cat skittles out the door between my legs. There on the floor is a beautiful piece of *lonza* covered in tell-tale teeth marks. I'm not sure who I am more scared for, the cat or me for letting it in, but instead my aunt, admittedly with a growl, adds that beautiful piece of homemade *lonza* to its bowl.

My brothers and I have always struggled to capture the tastes of Capoposta when at home. There is an essence of flavour that is impossible to replicate. For me, it's the vinegar. No matter how hard I try or what quality vinegar I buy, I cannot get a salad to taste like my aunt's. Zia Rosaria makes salad twice a day all year round so making vinegar is a fundamental part of their diet. She keeps her magic bottle handy under the sink, always at the ready. Upstairs in her attic, mixed in with the usual old furniture, school books, suitcases and other items she can't quite throw away, is a treasure trove of homemade food. There is a deep-freeze full of meat butchered from their or their relative's animals; salami, prosciutto and *lonza* stored in oil; chillies, onions, garlic and tomatoes hanging from the ceiling; potatoes, olive oil and, most importantly, the vinegar. Inside a huge glass flagon covered in dust and resting snug in a little manger is the vinegar mother. My aunt and uncle were given the vinegar mother as a wedding gift from my great uncle Brescio, who took it from his vinegar mother, whose ancestry is probably as long as that of the Di Sciascio clan.

When her little store under the sink is empty, my aunt climbs the stairs to the attic and takes some vinegar from this aged and weary flagon. The mother is constantly topped up with homemade wine that isn't worthy of serving at the table. My aunt uses white or red wine, it doesn't matter; the mother does her work and produces the most light, aromatic, fruity yet tangy vinegar imaginable. How I will miss her.

Rain brings a welcome break from olive picking and Zia Rosaria decides to make *pizzelle*, a cross between a waffle and pikelet that is particular to this area. Her brother pops over, as does our neighbour

Biasetto, and we sit together in the shed chatting while my aunt makes her *pizzelle* and Zio Alberto shaves over the shed sink. It is a lively and intimate gathering amongst people who have been sharing moments like this their whole lives.

Pizzelle are made only in Abruzzo and even then they differ slightly in different parts of the region. In some places they are crisp; in others they are soft and delicate. In our area of Abruzzo, *pizzelle* are soft and light. On special occasions they are rolled and filled with Italian crema (like our custard or pastry cream) or dipped in chocolate. They are absolutely beautiful and go perfectly with a strong espresso coffee. A good *pizzelle* leaves a fine film of oil on your hands and good eggs give them a beautiful rich golden colour.

You can't make these little gems without a *pizzelle* press. These come in two varieties: the old style, which is a cast iron press with long handles; or the new electric presses. The old presses are held over a naked flame on the stove or over hot coals in a hearth and this is still the preferred method of many Abruzzese women, including Zia Rosaria. Many of these presses were handmade to a pattern requested by the cook that included initials in the centre. When *pizzelle* are served, people know who has made them by the initials appearing on their surface. In times past women had to be careful to turn the press over at the correct time in order to ensure both sides of the *pizzelle* were cooked evenly. To do so they would hold the press over hot coals and pray the 'Our Father', then turn the press over and pray the 'Hail Mary', by which time the *pizzelle* was ready.

My dad absolutely loves *pizzelle* and often has one in his hand. He shares pieces with his grandchildren, especially Lulu, who searches out the *pizzelle* container as soon as she enters her grandparents' house. My mum uses an electric press, which is far more convenient. Finding a *pizzelle* press in Australia can be hard, but some specialty Italian importers do carry them. A standard electronic waffle maker can suffice, but the shape is not the same.

Pizzelle

The traditional recipe for *pizzelle* is one tablespoon of sugar, one tablespoon of olive oil and one tablespoon of flour for every egg, and a squeeze of lemon added to the batter. But really, every cook in our area has her own special adjustments. Less sugar will make them less sweet and substituting half the olive oil for seed or vegetable oil will make them lighter. A touch of *sambuca* added to the batter leaves a zing in your mouth, adding grated lemon rind as well as the juice makes them more tangy, and a *bustina di lievito* will make them light and fluffy. (In Italy, they don't use self-raising flour; instead they add little sachets of raising agent to plain flour. These sachets are called *bustina di lievito*.) You can find these at specialty Italian food stores.

Here is the recipe I saw my aunt use in the shed that
rainy day.

    12 free-range eggs
    6 tbspn sugar (don't follow the one spoon to
        one egg rule)
    8 tbspn canola or sunflower oil
    4 tbspn olive oil
    enough flour for the eggs
    a squeeze of lemon juice

Beat the eggs and sugar. Add oil and flour and lemon
juice. Whip by hand until it becomes an airy batter.
The batter should be like a pancake batter—not too
runny but not too thick.

Heat the *pizzelle* iron over a gas stove. Put a small
ladleful of mixture on the centre of the press and
close shut. Cook until slightly golden and *pizzelle* is
easily removed with a fork. The cooking time will
depend on your press. Usually the first two or three
aren't as nice as the rest of the batch.

Cool on a cake rack and store in an airtight cake tin.

Over the years my uncle's house been restored, reno-
vated and extended but the shell is still the rocks and
mortar that my ancestors put together, the house in
which my father was born. Next to my uncle's bedroom

is a small annexe that was a balcony when he and my dad were young. On the column in this annexe is a mirror. One day I ask my cousin why there is a mirror there. She tells me that when my dad was a young man he put a small broken piece of mirror on the balcony column so the men could use it while they shaved. Men from up and down the village would come to that balcony to shave with that mirror. When the house was renovated a couple of years ago, my uncle insisted that a mirror remain. It reminds him of his brother.

As I watch Zio Alberto shave over the shed sink, I think of Valentino. As my dad's Alzheimer's progresses he leaves patches of unshaved skin on his face and my mother now has to help him shave. Perhaps if he was here the men from the village would have done it for him in front of 'Valentino's mirror'.

It is now only five weeks until I leave Italy. I'm excited at the thought of going home but reflective about what I've learnt, experienced, tasted, tested, seen and achieved. Next year, though, is looking good. Yesterday on Italian television I watched with relief as Barack Obama was elected the new American president. It feels like watching history being made.

Winter

Arrivederci, Italia

I'M AT THE end of my journey. I've spent the last month and a half at Zio Alberto's house watching winter slowly arrive, the snow gradually covering the mountain as we celebrate the completion of the olive harvest. On my walks now I notice that the crops that were planted in October have sprouted with the autumn rains, the brown, ploughed fields softened by their tender green shoots. It's getting colder though; there has been snow close by and once more we sit around the fire in the shed as we did early in the year.

In one full cycle of the seasons I have traversed this remarkable country. Italy for me is a land of contrasts—language, character, architecture, climate, food and lifestyles vary from town to town and region to region. I've seen and experienced the Italy that tourists see, as well as been lucky enough to weave my way into the life of everyday Italians—those of the city living the rush of modern life, and those who rely on the sun, the earth and nature to chart their lives. I've been welcomed into people's homes and communities with such generosity and hospitality that at times I have been overwhelmed. But of all that I've seen, experienced, tasted, tested and pondered, Italy for me is family, food, *furbo* and father.

Family

I'm writing this in the house that my dad was born in. His father, uncles, grandfather and great uncles helped build this village that we now call Capoposta. They sacrificed many years working for others to bring the family out of poverty and buy the land that has sustained generations. They fought and died in world wars and had war appear on their doorstep. Families here live together in harmony, relying on each other for a living, comfort and laughter. Hours were and still are spent sitting around fires, huddled together in the warmth of the stables, toiling the land, preparing and sharing food, gathering water, weaving linen, sharing equipment, building furniture and tools, raising animals and rearing children. All of this, together.

There's a bond and closeness here. I see it when my dad's friends in Australia gather. I see it here in the way people speak of my father, a man some of them haven't seen in over fifty years. It's a familiarity with territory, land, and culture. They are bound by the history they share, a love for the mountain, valleys and fields of their land and by the stories they tell. And what stories they tell. Old people pass down the stories that were told to them by their parents and beyond. They are respected because of the history they carry within.

I feel blessed to be a part of that bond. I feel it in the way the people of my village smile when I knock on their door; the way they wave at me as I'm on my walks. I am Valentino's daughter staying with Alberto from Capoposta. I am a Di Sciascio. I am one of them and a little part of Valentino has come back. Their blue eyes that shine like mine, their round faces, their love and admiration for my dad and their genuine interest in my mum, my brothers and our life in Australia tells me I belong.

I make a passing comment about how generous my uncle has been. He looks at me seriously.

'What's your name?' he orders.

'Angela,' I reply.

'What's your surname?'

'Di Sciascio.'

'There is nothing more to say. You are one of us. What's mine is yours.'

Food

They say food is life. Here food is the centre of life, especially when shared with family. Food is more than all the wonderful tastes and recipes I have experienced and learnt. It is these people's attitude to food that has warmed both my heart and my stomach.

In Capoposta I have lived in a home where almost everything that is consumed is a product of the labour of that household. I've witnessed what it is to be close to nature, understood the simplicity this brings, and appreciated that if we want something good we have to work for it. Here the cycle of life is very apparent. Not everyone in Italy lives in this idyllic way, indeed even in tiny Capoposta only the older generation continues the subsistence lifestyle of their childhood, but there is still much to be learnt from it.

Zio Alberto and Zia Rosaria toil every day to keep this giant cycle of life turning. They rise at dawn, have coffee and begin their day with the care of the animals. The chickens, rabbits and pig are checked and fed, eggs collected, pens cleaned, and if needed, my aunt's strong arms and sharp knife end a life for our plate. The cattle that live in the same stable my dad kept warm in are fed, watered, cleaned and milked. Straw on the floor of the stable is changed twice a day, the dirty straw collected and kept in a huge compost mound for use at the end of summer to fertilise the fields. All the straw, hay for the cows, grain for the chooks is from their fields.

After this, Zia Rosaria heads for her vegetable garden, waters where necessary, plants when needed and harvests when ready. Now is the time for fennel, cabbage, *rapa* and beet, as well as the constant year-round supply of salad leaves. If she has killed a chicken or rabbit, she will skin, gut and prepare the meat for use. Only once all this is done do they sit down at the table to eat their breakfast of bread drizzled liberally with their own rich, green olive oil, sometimes sprinkled with their own paprika, and eaten with a glass of their wine and fruit. Zio Alberto will then head to the fields where he's either growing grain (most of which he sells; some he keeps for flour or food for the animals), growing hay for the animals, or pruning or harvesting olives for olive oil or grapes for wine.

My aunt spends the morning doing housework and preparing the main meal of the day. Lunch is big and wholesome, fit for kings and fuel for farmers. For *primo*, there is always pasta, sometimes homemade but usually De Cecco because it's made nearby from water and wheat they feel they know, and by people they do know. It is served with a tomato sauce made from preserved summer tomatoes, celery and herbs from her garden, onions and garlic harvested in summer and stored in her attic, and a serious amount of olive oil. When meat is used to flavour the sauce, it is lamb from a farm they know and trust, or veal from one of their own slaughtered calves. There's always a *secondo*, sometimes veal, sometimes rabbit, sometimes chicken, sometimes pork and very occasionally fish. The meat is never purchased, unless it's lamb. The *contorno* is usually salad or vegetables freshly picked from the garden that morning, drizzled with their oil and homemade vinegar. All followed by fruit and coffee.

My uncle returns to the fields in the afternoon and my aunt returns to her housework, sometimes to her vegetable garden, before preparing for the evening meal. Before dinner, the second cycle of animal rearing is completed. The pens are cleaned, animals fed and watered and cows milked. I hear my uncle and aunt talking to the cows as they do this together. Dinner is lighter than lunch, often just some salad, vegetables, bread and homemade cheese or salami. It may be a broth or a frittata or another meat dish. And so the cycle continues, every day, every season.

Admittedly most Italians live like you and me. Yet it is true that young children in Italy can describe food and flavours better than most adults in Australia. There are no children's menus in restaurants and they grow up eating all the flavours and ingredients that adults consume. People will spend twenty minutes discussing a menu before deciding and they will seek and get good advice from a waiter on what is fresh that day. Italians understand the seasons. They appreciate the history of their cuisine and shop in markets or from small vendors rather than supermarket chains when they can.

There are of course supermarkets here but in a large supermarket in Italy you may actually find a real fishmonger in the fish section, a real butcher who will cut meat to your request, a deli jam-packed with high-quality produce and definitely not all pre-cut. Shoppers wear plastic gloves to handle the fruit and vegetables and the deli assistants know how to cut, store and wrap cheese. Most Italians think large supermarkets are abhorrent but compared to ours they are heaven.

Things are changing in Italy. Package meals and pasta sauce in a jar are creeping into everyday life. There are McDonald's restaurants springing up, although most Italians still prefer a slice of pizza. Even so, the Italian appreciation of good food, of flavour, seasonal produce, quality ingredients and the ritual of sharing a meal together at a perfectly laid table will stay with me forever.

Furbo

According to my Italian dictionary, *furbo* means cunning, sly, astute. My cousin reckons that in order to survive in Italy, you need *furbo*. I agree. It is the essential difference between the Australian and Italian character. In Italy there is no shame in asking for a discount, and if you want advice you simply ask—it doesn't matter that there are other people waiting or indeed are in the middle of being served. When you need anything done, find a connection: the cousin of a friend or godmother of your neighbour's son-in-law, it doesn't really matter. Relationships and a connection, however loose, open doors, speed up procedures and get things done—or avoid things, depending upon your intention. Bureaucracy is rife in Italy so without *furbo*, you might spend the rest of your life paddling upstream.

Driving requires lots of *furbo*. Red lights, stop signs, pedestrian crossings and lines indicating your lane are simply suggestions. If you don't have *furbo* when driving in Italy, you don't move.

Furbo gives Italians a wonderful sense of confidence and alertness to their surroundings. They're quick-witted and conscious of all the connections that bind a people. It prevents a shyness but protects them from an openness that may expose them. It's feisty, protective, honest and entirely without self-consciousness.

Furbo is what makes Italians the people they are—it has helped them survive centuries of domination, discontent, war, hunger, feudalism and fascism. It has made them creative, inventive, resilient, reliant on those close to them and thick-skinned. *Furbo* lets them make the most of life amongst corruption, Mussolini, the monarchy, Garibaldi, over fifty governments in sixty years, Berlusconi, and organised crime. Without *furbo*, there would be no Italy as we know and love it.

Father

My dad is a wonderful man. He has passed on to his children the value of honest labour and a sense of pride, loyalty and respect for others. He was born in a time of hardship when the constraints of tradition, poverty and lack of work were a straightjacket on his adventurous spirit. So he embarked on a journey to a new land, a vast land with strange customs, attitudes, food and climate. He had to adapt to survive and thrive. He made a conscious decision to embrace Australia as his home even before he met my mother, and its way of life became his way of life. But inside he is still an Italian man from Capoposta. Valentino spent twenty-six years living amongst the people, homes, mountains, patchwork fields and valleys that is his Abruzzo. He was a music man who spent every available moment playing his accordion. He was a cheerful, hardworking, respectful man who had lots of friends. He was considerate of others and helped people when he could. He was part of the tight-knit community where everyone knew each other, watched out for each other, protected each other, laughed and cried together and even fed each other in times of need. He grew up with no shoes, no money, hardly any school, no trade, no electricity, no fresh running water and not much food. But his was a life filled with laughter, music, dancing, stories, family and friends. He was never alone; he was one of a group, a tribe. It's a tribe that still welcomes him home as one of their own even though he hasn't lived here for over fifty-six years. It's a tribe that has welcomed me with open arms.

I thank my father for the Italian identity that I love and hold dear. I do love this place and it will be hard for me to say goodbye, but I cannot live here. I am too much a fish out of water and I miss too much of home, our way of life and the people I cherish. I often teach my migrant students about culture shock. That it is real, a physical, emotional and at times overwhelming experience that they will all have to go through. Now I know that what I have been teaching is true, and I have a small glimmer of understanding about how my dad must have felt in his new country, how my students must feel, and how I feel about Australia and my home.

One day I am sitting in front of the fire in the shed with my uncle. We are discussing a phone call I had that morning with Mum. I tell him that calling home every day can be wonderful but that it also increases my homesickness. We wonder if Dad felt less or more homesick in his first years away from Italy when he could only communicate via letter or telegram. Zio recalls the first phone call he had with his brother. It was the early seventies and my Aunt Giuleitta had been the first in the family to get a telephone. They were talking about how nice it would be to speak to Valentino so my cousin Anna, who was three days old when my dad left, rang the operator in Rome, gave them our address and got connected through to Geelong. It was the middle of the night and at first my dad couldn't work out who had called him. He thought my cousin was in Australia and he asked where she was so he could go and pick her up. It was an unexpected experience for all and very emotional. Zio Alberto and Zia Giulietta were unable to speak through their tears. My mum remembers that Dad was unable to sleep afterwards.

I try to imagine what that phone call must have been like, to hear the voices of your siblings for the first time in nearly twenty years. Mum remembers Dad speaking to his sister Carmella and in the background he heard the sound of her wire door banging. For Dad, the sound of that door took him back to Capoposta and after he got off the phone he cried and cried. In this era of Facebook, Skype, phone cards and mobiles, it's impossible for me to imagine what he went through in those early days without constant contact with his family.

People sometimes ask me what I miss from home. I am surprised at what I do miss. I miss the sound of a wooden house. My house creaks under my feet, groans in the heat and shudders in the wind. It's almost a living entity. I miss the sound of Australian birds chirping madly in native trees. I miss the feel of the Australian sun on my skin. I miss red rock cliffs with an ocean beach. I miss walking barefoot, which is an absolute no-no in Italy, even in the house. I miss a long, straight, distant horizon. I miss cream—good, thick, fresh, artery-hardening cream. I miss, I miss …

The next time Dad asks Mum when I'm coming home, she replies, 'In two weeks!'

Home

As we drive down our street, I spot Dad out walking. We stop the car to surprise him but instead my presence only adds to his confusion; when we walk into the house with my bags, though, tears roll down his cheeks. He knows I am home. For eleven months he has been asking after me and now here we are standing together, embracing, silently weeping with happiness. My mum walks down the hallway with a big smile on her face. She has been awaiting my return as eagerly as Dad. It is so good to embrace my parents after such a long time apart. I am comforted, secure and safe in their arms.

When I left I was worried that Dad would not recognise me when I returned. Thankfully this is not so but I've only heard him speak a handful of English words since I got back. I feel blessed that at least I can now comprehend most of what he's saying to me in Italian. It doesn't always make sense and sometimes I can't work out who or what he's talking about but at least I can understand the words.

What I hadn't prepared myself for is the deterioration in my mother. She's had some health problems this year that have drained her energy and vitality. The constant caring for Dad has taken its toll and she has changed. Once a dynamo who ran a tight ship, now she is tired, sometimes grumpy, a little depressed and seemingly isolated from the world. She has a constant battle to care for a man who won't or can't accept that his illness requires care, and with this she has the added pressure of not being able to communicate with her husband in his language. She is losing control of her life and her body and resents having to rely on her children for help. It is heartbreaking to watch.

Sitting in the front room of my parents' house are Dad's three accordions. He plays regularly but not every day, some days better than others. His grandchildren dance around him when he does and his face lights up with pride and happiness.

I set out on my journey searching for Valentino, the man behind Wally, the man behind the father I know. What I have discovered is not a new and different father. The Valentino of Italy is the same loyal, strong, quiet, respectful and honest Wally that is my dad. His name may have changed and he may no longer play his accordion with the same grace, but my dad is Wally and he is Valentino. The man who fitted in to Australia, who married an Australian country girl, who ran a successful business, who is a constant in his children's lives is Wally—but Valentino made him. I like, respect and love them both. He should not be ashamed of Wally, nor feel like he left Valentino behind. They are one.